THE
PHILOSOPHY OF
J. S. MILL

JOHN STUART MILL, 1806-1873
By G. F. WATTS *in the National Portrait Gallery*

THE PHILOSOPHY OF J. S. MILL

BY

R. P. ANSCHUTZ

OXFORD
AT THE CLARENDON PRESS
1953

Oxford University Press, Amen House, London E.C.4

GLASGOW NEW YORK TORONTO MELBOURNE WELLINGTON
BOMBAY CALCUTTA MADRAS KARACHI CAPE TOWN IBADAN

Geoffrey Cumberlege, Publisher to the University

ACKNOWLEDGEMENTS

Most of Chapter IV and parts of Chapter VII of this book have appeared in an article in *Mind*; I am indebted to Professor Gilbert Ryle for permission to reprint these passages; I am more indebted to him for going over the whole typescript in detail. Dr. D. D. Raphael has also scrutinized the whole typescript and I am indebted to him for several valuable criticisms. To Dr. Elizabeth Sheppard I owe a vigorous attempt to make something readable out of my writing. Without my wife's help the manuscript would never have been typed nor, in all probability, written.

R. P. A.

AUCKLAND UNIVERSITY COLLEGE

NEW ZEALAND

November 1951

CONTENTS

I

INTRODUCTION

1. MILL began to be a force in English life and philosophy rather more than a hundred years ago. At the beginning of this period, say between 1840 and 1860, he was, as Herbert Spencer puts it, 'the one conspicuous figure in the higher regions of thought'. Jevons was still complaining in the seventies that Mill's opinions were quoted on every subject of social importance, 'as if they were the oracles of a perfectly wise and logical mind'. Nor was it until the beginning of the nineties that Bradley could congratulate himself that there was 'no established reputation', meaning Mill's, 'which now does much harm in philosophy'. When, however, it did begin to decline Mill's prestige went with astonishing rapidity and completeness; and in the field of philosophy at least, he has not so far figured among the rehabilitated Victorians.

Some of the reasons for Mill's loss of reputation are clear enough. In the sixties he was incapable of the intense intellectual energy that had produced the *Logic* and the *Political Economy* in the forties. Although he continued to be persuasive enough in review articles and in essays on circumscribed themes, he failed to make a success of the *Examination of Hamilton*, where he attempted to cover the whole field of philosophy. Unlike the majority of men, again, Mill did not mellow in his old age; as a consequence there was no great desire in some quarters to do justice to him when he died;[1]

---

[1] *The Times* actually went so far as to quote an early squib of Thomas Moore's in its obituary notice by way of reminding its readers of Mill's adolescent activities as an advocate of birth control.

'There are two Mr. Mills, too, whom those who like reading
What's vastly unreadable, call very clever;
And whereas Mill Senior makes war on *good* breeding,
Mill Junior makes war on all breeding whatever.'

B

and his reputation suffered a further blow with the post-humous publication of his *Autobiography* and of his *Three Essays on Religion*. The former was regarded by his opponents as confirming the suspicion that he was merely a 'manufactured man'—made by his father in the image of Bentham; his friends were chilled to discover in the latter that his views on religion were considerably less inflexible than they had allowed themselves to believe.

So far as Mill's popular reputation was concerned, however, the overriding fact which made these various occurrences important is the radical change that overtook the Victorian mood in the sixties. In the forties, as Matthew Arnold described the situation, everything was seen by the young and ardent, as it was seen by Mill, 'in inseparable connection with politics and practical life'; but during the sixties the young began to feel that they had 'pretty well exhausted the benefits of seeing things in this connection'. Under the guidance of Arnold and Pater and later of Wilde they began to 'try a more disinterested mode of seeing them'. Naturally enough, Mill's essay on *Liberty* continued to be generally read and approved. But in regard to the rest of his work, the comments tend to be supercilious. 'Poor dear Mill,' says a character in *Belchamber*, 'it is a pity he is so *vieux jeu*; he had such a nice refined face, and learned Greek as a baby, and it was so nice and unconventional of him to want women in parliament. Perhaps in time parliament may come to be all women, and men be free to look after things that really matter.'

2. In the academic sphere, Mill's fate has been rather different. At first sight he is the most lucid of philosophers. Many people have spoken of the marvellous intelligibility of his writing; some have even mentioned the intellectual ecstasy produced in them by the exact and ordered sequence of his reasoning. Usually, however, it is not long before doubts begin to creep in. Although the lucidity remains, its span is

seen to be somewhat limited. It extends to paragraphs and to chapters, sometimes even to whole essays. But there are often awkward breaks between paragraphs and chapters in his longer books and one sometimes has the uneasy feeling that he is being equally lucid on both sides of a question. Weasel words and phrases—*experience, individuality, advanced thinker, permanent possibilities of sensation*—suddenly loom large and become more inscrutable the longer one looks at them. Hence it has been generally held, since Jevons first made the discovery, that Mill's mind was 'essentially illogical' and that his philosophy was notable mainly for its 'intricate sophistry'.

Oddly enough, however, this judgement has not led to Mill's neglect in academic circles. Nobody now talks of Hamilton or Whewell; but Mill's name continually crops up in philosophical discussions. There is no one, I imagine, except Aristotle, who is more frequently referred to in logic textbooks. This is partly due to the fact that Mill offers a body of doctrine and a set of technical terms on the subject of induction which have proved extremely useful in the classroom. But a more important reason is that he has come to be regarded as a sort of personification of certain tendencies in philosophy which it is regarded as continually necessary to expose. Thus he is, or says he is, a utilitarian; yet nothing, it is pointed out, could tell more strongly against utilitarianism than certain passages in his writings. Then again he is said to be an empiricist (without his authority) and his theories of the syllogism and of mathematics are constantly used to demonstrate the fatal consequences of this way of thinking.

3. Philosophical discussion would be a good deal more colourless and long-winded than it has any right to be if we could not link the name of a well-known philosopher in this sort of way with some important doctrine. We are, of course, paying a considerable compliment to any man when we do so, since we are saying, in effect, that he has worked out the

implications of the doctrine more fully and explicitly than anybody else. But at the same time we also run a considerable risk of misunderstanding him, for we can scarcely help interpreting everything he says in the light of his presumed realism or scepticism or whatever it is; and it has been generally acknowledged in the case of more than one philosopher (Locke's is a particularly pertinent case here) that a traditional label, applied as often as not in the interests of party politics, has resulted in a very distorted view of his teaching.

Now it appears to me at least as misleading to talk without qualification of Mill's empiricism as of Locke's empiricism. In the writings of both men, it is true, genuinely empiricist doctrines are to be found, but in both cases they are accompanied by other doctrines that cannot be regarded as empiricist by any stretch of definition. Thus the theory of the syllogism usually associated with Mill's name is, I should say, an empiricist theory but not the theory of induction. The characteristic feature of the former is the assertion that we can never attain certainty in our reasonings, because we must always argue from particulars to particulars. The underlying assumption is that we can never establish any real connexion between particulars by way of universals because *universals are merely collections of particulars*. The theme of the latter, on the contrary, is that we can obtain certainty by way of scientific experiment because the *particulars* we are dealing with there *are merely collections of universals* It is on this assumption that the problem of induction is reduced by Mill to the formal one of determining what universals in one particular are connected with what universals in another; and it is this problem which he solves by means of his Canons of Induction.

It is equally misleading in my opinion to speak without qualification of Mill's utilitarianism. If we do we immediately suggest that there is a degree of agreement between the ethical and political doctrines of Bentham and Mill which does not on the face of it exist. Nor is it sufficient to add that Mill modified the utilitarianism he inherited from Bentham and his father in this way and that, in order to meet the criticisms it encountered in Victorian times. He does, it is true, sometimes give that impression (as in his essay on *Utilitarianism*); but elsewhere (as in his essay on *Liberty*) he scarcely attempts to conceal the fact that his premisses are completely independent of Bentham's.

4. Thus, contrary to the common belief, I should say that it is very hazardous to characterize offhand the precise position of Mill on any major philosophical topic. All his theories, like Locke's, are extremely complex and unstable structures, prone to fall to pieces at the first inconvenient question. Nevertheless there are one or two points about him which leap to the eye and by their aid it is, I think, possible to unravel to some degree the tangled skein of his thought.

For one thing, Mill was not the paragon of the middle-class virtues that he is sometimes represented as being. 'Circumspect on principle,' says Halévy, 'and very much concerned to escape the accusation of being either exclusive or fanatical.' But in fact he often behaved with a reckless disregard of consequences more suitable to a romantic than to a utilitarian. He is thoroughly romantic, again, and thoroughly representative of his age, in the eagerness with which he seeks out and endeavours to assimilate every last exotic line of thought which shows any signs of vitality. He himself claimed to be superior to most of his contemporaries in 'ability and willingness to learn from everybody'; and indeed, for all his father's careful schooling there was never anybody less buttoned up against alien influences than Mill. Somewhere or other in his writings you can discern traces of every wind that blew in the early nineteenth century.

On the other hand there was another strain in Mill which was perpetually at war with this. He was an inveterate systematizer and, search as he might, he never succeeded in finding a system which had anything like the appeal of the one he had been brought up in. Thus for all his open-mindedness it is of the first importance in trying to understand him that we should understand Bentham and James Mill, since it was within the framework provided by them that he tried to organize the new truths that he discovered for himself.

5. Now just as communism claims to be the scientific political theory of our time, so did radicalism claim to be the scientific political theory of the early nineteenth century; and neither claim can be lightly dismissed. In one sense of the term Marxism is scientific and so, in another, is Benthamism. But in either case it is obviously essential to know exactly what is meant by science, and, as Halévy has shown with great particularity, we have to refer back to the work of Newton to understand what Bentham meant by it.

Granted [says Halévy], a science of the mind and of society which exhibits the qualities both of the experimental and of the exact sciences, analogous to the physics of Newton, should it not be possible to found on these new disciplines a moral and legal theory which should be scientific—the achievement of the universal practical science? Such is the problem which exercised thinking people in England throughout Bentham's century. What is known as utilitarianism or philosophical radicalism can be defined as nothing but an attempt to apply the principles of Newton to the affairs of politics and of morals.[1]

Thus there were two strains in Mill. The sensitive temperament, that craved for sympathetic support and responded so delicately to every trend of the age was balanced, or almost balanced, by a strong and thoroughly trained will which was never content to absorb influences but always persisted in systematizing them from a radical point of view, that is, from a point of view which had in it something of the moralist but a good deal more of the scientist. If the study of Mill's philosophy is approached with these points in mind it may be

[1] Halévy, *Growth of Philosophical Radicalism*, p. 6.

found, I suggest, that it is not entirely the congeries of intricate sophistry that it appeared to Jevons. Or if that impression still persists, it should at any rate be clear that the explanation is not to be found solely in the illogicality of Mill's mind. Looking back upon the stormy period of his youth Mill subsequently said of himself: 'I found the fabric of my old and taught opinions giving way in many fresh places and I never allowed it to fall to pieces but was incessantly occupied in weaving it anew';[1] and this is a description that never really ceased to be applicable to him.

[1] *Autobiography* (World's Classics), p. 132.

THE PRINCIPLES OF UTILITY
AND OF INDIVIDUALITY

1. ALTHOUGH Mill's previous education had been, in a way, a course in Benthamism, he records that the first few pages of Bentham he ever read burst upon him with all the force of novelty. The pages which so impressed him were those at the beginning of *The Principles of Morals and Legislation*, in which Bentham passes judgement upon the common modes of moral reasoning deduced from phrases like *the law of nature*, *right reason*, *the moral sense*, and so on, and denounces them as dogmatism in disguise. 'They consist all of them', he says, 'in so many contrivances for avoiding the obligation of appealing to any standard and for prevailing upon the reader to accept of the author's opinion as a reason for itself.' In the presence of this passage the feeling rushed upon Mill 'that all previous moralists were superseded and that here indeed was the commencement of a new era of thought'.[1]

If now we turn to Bentham we find an equally explicit statement of his indebtedness to Hume, and, more particularly, to the third volume of Hume's *Treatise of Human Nature*. Bentham owned, indeed, to sharing the common opinion that the first two volumes, and perhaps even part of the third, might well be dispensed with. But after all retrenchments had been made, there remained enough, he considered, to have laid mankind under 'indelible obligations' to Hume, in that he had effectually destroyed the fiction of the original contract and had demonstrated with the strongest force of evidence 'that the foundations of all *virtue* are laid in Utility'; and he concludes with a tribute to Hume very

[1] *Autobiography*, p. 54.

similar to Mill's tribute to him. 'For my part', he says, 'I well remember; no sooner had I read that part of the work which touches on this subject, than I felt as if scales had fallen from my eyes. I then, for the first time, learned to call the cause of the people the cause of Virtue.'[1]

From these two very deliberate and detailed statements it would appear, then, that the course of English political and ethical theory, in one of its branches at least, runs in a straight line from Hume to Bentham and from Bentham to Mill. Hume, it seems, had demolished the theories of natural law and social contract which had dominated European thought from the days of the Greek philosophers and Roman lawyers; he had erected in their stead the simple principle of utility; and it had been left to Bentham, and then to Mill, to apply this principle to the various departments of government and of life.

2. Nor can there by any doubt that there is a good deal of truth in this account. It was in the seventeenth century, with the rise of the physical sciences, that the decisive break with traditional ideas was made in most branches of philosophy. But for some reason or other (perhaps because the seventeenth century was able to use the traditional political ideas in a revolutionary way) that break was postponed in the case of political theory until the eighteenth century. Hence, for instance, the astonishing contrast between Locke's *Essay on the Human Understanding* and his *Essays on Government*. In the former he is a pioneer and presents us with the problems with which we are still struggling; but in the latter he is a complete conservative, content for the most part with the solutions of St. Thomas Aquinas.

When, however, the break did come, it divided philosophers into two schools of thought regarding politics, quite as sharply as the break in the seventeenth century had divided them into two schools regarding epistemology. On the one side

[1] Bentham, *Fragment on Government*, chap. i, par. 36, footnote.

are the organic theories of Rousseau, Hegel, and Marx who stressed the importance of the general will and sought guidance from the march of history; on the other, the utilitarian theories of Hume, Bentham, and Mill who regarded all forms of social organization as a means of securing the happiness of individuals; and, broadly speaking, the main interest of modern political theory lies in the fight between these two schools of political thought, in which the clash between Mill and Carlyle was one incident.

But although it is essential to the understanding of Mill's political position to stress the fact that it developed within this framework, it is also important to notice that this framework is not nearly so rigid as he sometimes makes out. As against Rousseau, Hegel, and Marx, we may say, Hume, Bentham, and Mill are all utilitarians. Nevertheless the principles of utility actually acknowledged by these men are very different propositions. In some respects, indeed, Mill shows a definite tendency to revert to something very like the doctrine of natural rights and social contract which Hume and Bentham began by denying.

3. The readiness with which Bentham is prepared to dispense with two-thirds of Hume's *Treatise* may, perhaps, raise some suspicion that they are not entirely at one over the remaining third. When we consider the grounds on which the two men recommend the principle of utility we find that they are widely at variance. For Hume, 'virtue is distinguished by the pleasure and vice by the pain that any action, sentiment or character gives us by the mere view and contemplation'. Thus the central problem of ethics, as he sees it, reduces to the question: what characters afford us this sort of pleasure?; and he comes to the conclusion that we derive it 'from the view of a character which is naturally fitted to be useful to others, or to the person himself, or which is agreeable to others or to the person himself'.[1]

[1] Hume, *Treatise*, iii. 1. 2; iii. 3. 1.

Bentham, however, is concerned with a completely different problem. 'What one expects to find in a principle', he says, 'is something that points out some external consideration as a means of warranting and guiding the internal sentiments of approbation and disapprobation'; and it is on the ground that utility, and utility alone, provides such a principle that he urges its acceptance. 'Of an action that is conformable to the principle of utility', he thinks, 'one may always say either that it is one that ought to be done; or at least that it is not one that ought not to be done.' When thus interpreted, accordingly, the words *ought* and *right* and *wrong* and others of that stamp have a meaning; when otherwise, they have none.[1]

Thus it seems clear that there is a fundamental difference between the utilitarianism of Hume and that of Bentham. Hume offers the principle of utility as a description of received morality, Bentham as a standard by which it should be judged. It is because of their different conceptions of the role of the principle of utility that Hume could be a Tory while Bentham and Mill were bound to be reformers; that is also why Hume's idea of the sort of proof appropriate to the principle of utility differs so completely from that of Bentham and Mill; and that, again, is why the theories of utility and of moral sense were complementary for Hume but contradictory for Bentham and Mill.

4. Having discovered that we do in fact approve of actions which promote the general happiness, whether or not they also promote our own, Hume asks why we approve of them; and he comes to the obvious conclusion that, along with self-love, we also have a 'feeling for the happiness of mankind and a resentment of their misery', which he calls the 'moral sentiment'. Bentham, however, thinks of the principle of utility not as one that we ordinarily do obey but simply as one that we ought to obey.

[1] Bentham, *Principles of Morals and Legislation*, chap. 2, par. 12; chap. 1, par. 10.

On the other hand, Bentham finds that the standing difficulty in the way of persuading people to apply the principle of utility is that they prefer to rely, quite uncritically, on the pronouncements of their untutored consciences. Hence to tell them that they have a moral sense, even if it is supposed to be directed towards the greatest happiness of the greatest number, is, in his opinion, to encourage their delusions of self-sufficiency and discourage any attempt to examine the actual consequence of their actions. Thus Bentham considered that all the antagonists of utilitarianism, as he understood it, might be lumped together as champions of the moral sense in one form or another; and for the next hundred years most British moralists, whether they accepted Bentham's teaching or not, were content to accept these as the alternatives before them.

According to Whewell, for instance, who was probably the most influential of the academic opponents of utilitarianism in the early nineteenth century, 'Schemes of morality are of two kinds—those which assert it to be the law of human action to aim at some external object like Pleasure or Utility or the Greatest Happiness of the Greatest Number and those which would regulate human action by an internal principle as Conscience or a Moral Faculty or Duty or Rectitude.' Mill is merely stating the orthodox radical argument in favour of the former alternative when he maintains that it alone enables an appeal to be made 'from a received opinion, however generally entertained, to the discussions of cultivated reason'. It is, again, entirely in the spirit of Bentham that Mill goes on to charge Whewell with pandering to the interests of hierarchies by providing, in his intuitionist system of ethics, 'an apparatus for converting prevailing opinions in matters of morality into reasons for themselves'.[1]

5. It is not, however, a matter merely of asserting that the

[1] Whewell, *Lectures on the History of Moral Philosophy*, pp. 1 f., (condensed); Mill, *Dissertations*, i. 158.

theory of utility is capable of a precise objective application, while the theory of the moral sense is not. It is also necessary to make good the assertion by actually applying the theory. But this is not possible, as Bentham realized from the beginning, by means of the principle of utility alone; and in fact he achieved his results by means of three interlocking principles, with the last of which, in particular, Mill found himself in the sharpest disagreement.

According to the first of Bentham's principles, which may be called the principle of individualism, any question regarding political or social affairs is reducible immediately and without remainder to a question regarding individual men and women. 'The community', he says, 'is a fictitious body, composed of the individual persons who are considered as constituting, as it were, its *members*. The interest of the community then is What?—the sum of the interests of the several persons who compose it.'[1]

In the second place, having reduced the interests of the community to the sum of the interests of its several members, Bentham now considers by what standard he is to judge of the extent by which their interests are promoted or thwarted by any action. Here, again, according to Bentham the answer is extremely simple, so simple indeed that one is sometimes tempted to wonder whether it is not merely verbal. 'The greatest happiness of all those whose interest is in question', he says, 'is the right and proper and only right and proper and universally desirable end of human action.' This is the principle of utility or, as Bentham afterwards preferred to call it, the greatest happiness principle.[2]

Bentham does, however, recognize that there is some vagueness about this notion of happiness and in his third step he endeavours, by means of the principle of the felicific calculus, to make it precise. The happiness or unhappiness of anybody,

[1] Bentham, *Principles of Morals and Legislation*, chap. 1, par. 4.
[2] Ibid., chap. 1, par. 1, footnote.

he now assumes, is always reducible to an algebraic sum of pleasures and pains. All that we need to do, therefore, to measure the happiness of any individual (and hence the well-being of any community) is to tot up the values of his various pleasures and pains, counting the pleasures as plus and the pains as minus. Consequently Bentham issues minute instructions, on which he regards 'the whole fabric of morals and legislation' as finally resting, for estimating the value of each pleasure and each pain.[1]

Thus by means of these three principles—of individualism, of utility or greatest happiness, and of the felicific calculus—it is possible, according to Bentham, to reduce the vague generalities of politics to precise quantitative statements. Regarded in this way there is a certain analogy, much treasured by the philosophical radicals, between the procedure advocated by Bentham in the social sciences, and that which is actually followed in the physical sciences. According to the first principle, all questions regarding society are reduced to questions regarding individual persons; according to the second, all questions regarding individuals are reduced to questions regarding their happiness; according to the third, all questions regarding happiness are reduced to questions regarding measurable pleasures and pains. As a grand consequence of the whole it follows, therefore, that the rightness or wrongness of any action, public or private, may be precisely determined by making the appropriate calculations regarding its probable consequences in the way of pleasure–pain, and contrasting the balance thus obtained with the balance obtained by any alternative course of action.

6. These same principles of reduction, moreover, become relevant again when it is a question of deciding not what ends the community should aim at but what means should be employed to obtain them. In this case, the problem of the legislator is a matter, to use a later phrase, of social engineer-

[1] Bentham, *Principles of Morals and Legislation*, chap. 4, par. 2, footnote.

ing, that is, of so arranging the relations between individuals that when each acts according to his own interests they will inevitably produce the desired result by their various interactions. Bentham provides a specimen of the utilitarian treatment of this sort of topic in his theory of punishment. James Mill provides another, which greatly exercised his son, in his theory of government.[1]

The question of government, according to James Mill, is a question of the adaptation of means to an end subject to a standing difficulty. The end is to obtain 'the greatest possible happiness of society by insuring to every man the greatest possible quantity of the produce of his labour'. And this object, it is generally agreed, can best be attained when a great number of men combine and delegate to a small number the power necessary for protecting them all. The difficulty, however, is that these men may, and usually do, take advantage of their power to despoil those whom they are supposed to protect. Thus the problem of government, in the opinion of James Mill, reduces to this—how are we to restrain those in whose hands are lodged the powers necessary for the protection of all from making bad use of it? Consequently it is to this problem that he devotes the greater part of his *Essay on Government*.

It was, to begin with, quite clear to James Mill, as it was to all the utilitarians, that power always corrupts. For although they recognized benevolence (along with malevolence) as one of the springs of human behaviour, they were convinced that men are for the most part moved by the various forms of self-interest. What is true of any individual they also held to be true (and even truer) of any class of individuals. Hence James Mill infers that 'there is no individual or combination of individuals, except the community itself, who would not have an interest in bad government, if entrusted with its

---

[1] James Mill, *Essay on Government*. The following paragraphs summarize the argument of Sects. i to vi which constitute about half the *Essay*.

powers'. To this he adds that 'the community itself is incapable of exercising the powers of government and must entrust them to some individual or combination of individuals'; and from these premises he draws the conclusion that the representative system offers the only possible hope of good government, since it is only under this system that the governed are able to refuse re-election to any member of the government who prefers his own interest to theirs.

Thus we have here, according to J. S. Mill's analysis of his father's argument, 'a fundamental theorem of political science, consisting of three syllogisms, and depending chiefly on two general premises'. In the first step, it is asserted that men's actions are always determined by their interests and by their interests is understood their private, worldly, or personal interests. In the second step, it is inferred that as the actions of mankind are determined by their selfish interests, the only rulers who will govern in the interests of the governed are those whose own interests are in accordance with them. In the third step, it is added that accountability to the governed is the only cause capable of producing in the rulers a sense of identity of interest with the ruled. Hence, as a result of the whole, it is concluded 'that the desire of retaining or the fear of losing their power is the sole motive which can be relied on for producing on the part of rulers a course of conduct in accordance with the general interest'.[1]

7. In his most deliberate characterization of Bentham, Mill gives it as his opinion that he was possessed 'both of remarkable endowments for philosophy and of remarkable deficiencies for it'. He was fitted, beyond almost anybody, to draw from his premises conclusions which were not only correct but precise and practicable; but his 'lot was cast in a generation of the leanest and barrenest men whom England had yet produced and he was an old man before a better race came in'. Consequently his experience had furnished him

[1] *Logic*, vi. 8. 3.

with a remarkably slender stock of premises regarding human nature; and the root of all his deficiencies, Mill considered, was to be found in his conception of man as a being governed in all his conduct partly by self-interest, partly by sympathies, or occasionally antipathies, towards other people but never by any idea of 'spiritual perfection'.

It is, however, precisely this idea, according to Mill, that lies at the root of any morality which aims to do more than prescribe 'some of the more obvious dictates of worldly prudence and outward probity and beneficence'; consequently Bentham's philosophy, which finds no place for such notions as conscience, self-respect, and honour, has little to offer the individual in his great task of self-education and character formation; and Mill adds that it has not much more to offer society.

It will [he says], enable a society which has attained a certain state of spiritual perfection (and the maintenance of which in that society is otherwise provided for) to prescribe the rules by which it may protect its material interests. It will do nothing (except sometimes as an instrument in the hands of a higher doctrine) for the spiritual interests of society.[1]

Now, as Mill himself notes, this passage was written at the height of his reaction against Bentham and he does not again indulge in such plain speaking about him. But this does not mean that he abandoned the opinion expressed here. It merely means that he had come to the conclusion that Bentham's philosophy 'as an instrument of progress' had been to some extent discredited before it had done its work and that to lend a hand towards lowering its reputation further was to do 'more harm than service to improvement'.[2] Henceforth, accordingly, he systematically slurred over the respects in which he differed from Bentham and insisted, to the point of disingenuousness, upon the respects in which they agreed, so that they might

---

[1] *Dissertations*, i. 355–66.   [2] *Autobiography*, p. 185.

present a united front against conservatism and reaction; and this, I believe, explains a good deal that at first sight is extremely puzzling in Mill's statements about the principle of utility.

8. It is, for example, notorious that in his essay on *Utilitarianism* Mill interprets the principle of utility in such a way that it cannot possibly be used as Bentham proposed to use it. 'Utility or the Greatest Happiness Principle', Mill tells us, 'holds that actions are right in proportion as they tend to promote happiness, wrong as they tend to promote the reverse of happiness.' Like Bentham, again, Mill understands, or says he understands, by happiness, 'pleasure and the absence of pain'. But whereas Bentham refused to recognize any but quantitative differences between pleasures and pains, Mill also recognizes qualitative differences. Thus, at one stroke Mill destroys the whole basis of the felicific calculus upon which Bentham relied for the application of the principle of utility; and it becomes then quite impossible, on any lines envisaged by Bentham, at least, to decide which of several alternative courses of action is likely to produce the greatest amount of happiness.

Nor is this all. The assertion that certain kinds of pleasure are more valuable than others is coupled by Mill with the assertion that certain kinds of people are more valuable than others, because they are capable of the more valuable kinds of pleasure; and then having reached this point he decides that, as they are capable of the more valuable pleasures, it is immaterial whether they actually obtain them. 'It is better', he says in a much-quoted sentence, 'to be a human being dissatisfied than a pig satisfied; better to be Socrates dissatisfied than a fool satisfied.' Thus it begins to be evident that the utilitarianism, if it can be called utilitarianism, in which Mill really believes has little to do with happiness and nothing at all with pleasure.[1]

---

[1] *Utilitarianism*, chap. 2, 5th ed., p. 14.

Now, according to the legend which has grown up about Mill in academic circles, he was a fair-minded but obtuse man who was apt to make concessions to his opponents without perceiving how fatal they were to his own theories; and such passages as these are frequently cited as prime examples of these characteristics. But although the confusion here is undeniable it has, I think, to be explained along different lines. After his period of youthful revolt there were two elements in Mill's ethical and political thinking. One is represented in its purest form by the essay on *Whewell* where he is an orthodox Benthamite, the other by the essay on *Liberty* where he is not; and the real charge that lies against Mill, I believe, is that for purely political reasons (for he is certainly not the disinterested man of the academic legend) he never made any serious attempt to distinguish them. Hence, naturally enough, the inconsistencies in the essay on *Utilitarianism* where both doctrines are developed together.

What then is the 'higher doctrine' in which Mill really believed and by means of which he hoped to make good the deficiencies of Bentham's utilitarianism? It may be called, as Mill sometimes calls it, 'the principle of individuality' or 'the principle of the sovereignty of the individual'.[1] But it is to be sharply distinguished from Bentham's principle of individualism. The meaning of that is entirely transitional and factual; it asserts that the community is merely an appearance (or as he says, 'a fictitious entity') whose reality consists entirely in the individual persons who are said to be its members. It leads to the further assertion, in the principle of utility, that the important thing about individual persons from an ethical point of view is their happiness, which Bentham regarded as a state which they passively suffer; and this interpretation is rendered precise when happiness is reduced, according to the principle of felicific calculus, to a sum of pleasures and pains. Thus in the second and third of

[1] *Autobiography*, p. 217.

his principles of reduction Bentham is saying, in effect, that as a community is reducible to the individuals who are said to be its members, so also are the individuals reducible, at least for the purposes of morals and legislation, to the pleasures and pains which they are said to suffer.

What Mill, on the other hand, is mostly concerned to emphasize in his moral and political teaching is the reality and importance of 'human liberty and spontaneity'. Thus his principle of individuality, unlike Bentham's principle of individualism, is final and normative. In asserting the reality of human individuality, Mill denies its reducibility to pleasures and pains or to anything else; in asserting the absolute importance of self-development he identifies the well-being of the individual with a sort of well-doing very different from the passive happiness of Bentham; and thus he is led to a variety of conclusions quite remote from anything contemplated by the older generation of utilitarians.

9. Of what value then is this principle of individuality by means of which Mill hoped to make good the deficiencies of the principle of utility? In its widest sense, the notion of individuality is similar to Hegel's notion of personality. An individual, to begin with, is something *in* himself—something indivisible or, at any rate, irreducible—and then, again, he is or, rather, becomes something *for* himself. Understood in this sense, then, the principle of individuality will emphasize the importance of those reflexive operations—self-development, self-improvement, self-formation, self-respect, conscience, and honour—which the older utilitarians had neglected; and so far as this is his meaning, Mill's teaching must be regarded as a decided improvement upon theirs.

Everybody was well enough aware at this time of a tremendous stirring among the unprivileged classes. But most of the privileged were concerned either to subdue this unrest or to divert it to their own ends. Mill was one of the few who accepted and respected it at its face value, as evincing a determination on the part of the unprivileged to become something for themselves and not merely for the privileged.

The poor [he says in one of his most noteworthy utterances] have come out of leading strings and cannot any longer be governed and treated like children. To their own qualities must now be commended the care of their destiny. Modern nations will have to learn the lesson that the well-being of a people must exist by means of the justice and self-government of the individual citizens.[1]

To Mill's credit, again, must be placed his constant insistence on the superiority of the active type of character over the passive. His reasons for maintaining this, in face of the common belief in the virtue of contentment, exhibit him, moreover, as possessing an insight into the subtler recesses of the human heart with which he is seldom credited.

The person [he says], bestirring himself with hopeful prospects to improve his own circumstances, is the one who feels good-will towards others engaged in the same pursuit. But those who, while desiring what others possess, put no energy into striving for it, are either incessantly grumbling that fortune does not do for them what they do not attempt to do for themselves or overflowing with envy and ill-will towards those who possess what they would like to have.[2]

Thus Mill arrives at the conclusion that a great deal of seeming contentment is 'real discontent combined with indolence or self-indulgence, which while taking no legitimate means of raising itself, delights in bringing others down to its own level'. Estimating this as one of the principal reasons for the failure of other nations to enter into the general movement of European progress he evinces a decided preference, despite all their failings, for the striving go-ahead character of England and the United States, and this indeed is a theme

---

[1] *Political Economy*, iv. 17. 2.
[2] *Representative Government*, chap. 3, 3rd ed., p. 61.

of which he never tires. 'Inactivity, unaspiringness, absence of desire', in his opinion, 'are a much more fatal hindrance to improvement than any misdirection of energy.' 'It is not', he says elsewhere, 'because men's desires are strong that they act ill; it is because their consciences are weak. Energy may be turned to bad uses, but more good may always be made of an energetic character, than of an indolent and impassive one.'[1]

10. There is also another respect in which Mill's teaching on the subject of individuality is on the whole (for he has his lapses) of considerable value. In the wide sense just explained, the notion of individuality or self-development is a purely formal one which stresses the necessity for men to become something for themselves but provides no information as to what that should be. If then this notion is to be regarded as a complete guide to conduct a content has somehow to be provided for it; and it has often appeared to those who value the notion that the way to do this is to take advantage of a completely different meaning of self-development in which the direction of the development is supposed to be indicated by the potentialities of the self.

Regarded in this way, self-development becomes an entirely subjective and an entirely affirmative process. To begin with, we have to determine the potentialities of the particular self we are dealing with and then we have to stand aside and provide room for their maturation. Thus the development of individuality is to be all a matter of freedom and spontaneity —of unfolding as a flower unfolds—unhindered by anything in the way of training or self-denial; and prompted, perhaps, by bitter memories of the training he had received from his father this is how Mill sometimes speaks of it. 'Human nature', he says for example, 'is not a machine to be built after a model and set to do exactly the work prescribed for it, but a tree which requires to grow and develop itself on all sides

[1] *Representative Government*, chap. 3, pp. 61 ff.; *Liberty*, chap. 3, p. 107.

according to the tendency of the inward forces which make it a living thing.'[1]

At other times, however (and reversals of this kind are not uncommon with Mill), there is no one who is more energetic in his protests against this sort of theory. It cannot, he points out, be interpreted literally because it would then imply that we have to approve of everything that has ever been done by anybody. Hence a distinction is commonly drawn between that part of a man's conduct which is done with deliberation and that part which is done from impulse. 'The result is the vein of sentiment so common in the modern world (though unknown to the philosophical ancients) which exalts instinct at the expense of reason.' And this is a result with which Mill has no sympathy. 'It is only', he holds, 'in a highly artificial-ised condition of human nature that the notion could have grown up that goodness is natural; because only after a long course of artificial education did good sentiments become so predominant over bad as to arise unprompted when occasion called for.' Indeed he pursues this line of thought so far as to represent the good life in terms of a revolt against nature— internal as well as external. 'The duty of man', he says, 'is the same in respect to his own nature as in respect to the nature of all other things, namely not to follow but to amend it. . . . The artificially created, or at least artificially perfected, nature of the best and noblest human beings, is the only nature which it is ever commendable to follow.'[2]

Nor can there by any doubt, as Morley shows very clearly, that these sentiments are thoroughly congruous with Mill's fundamental ethical convictions.

Mr. Mill [Morley says] inherited from Turgot and Condorcet the idea of perfectibility. This is the key alike to the *Liberty*, the *Utilitarianism* and some of the most original chapters in the *Political Economy*. To bring this conviction of the immense improvableness both of the arrangements of society and of the

[1] Ibid.   [2] *Three Essays on Religion*, 3rd ed., pp. 46, 54.

character of man into a leading place among our political notions and most active inspirations, it is necessary to displace the meta-physical idea of Nature as a force presiding over the destinies of humanity and benignly shaping them to higher and more pros-perous ends. And this exhibition must be what Mr. Mill has made it, a demonstration of triumphs over Nature, if we use the word to describe all that takes place spontaneously without the voluntary intervention of man, including man's own primitive impulses.[1]

11. The question still, however, remains: which of our impulses are we to develop and which to starve?; and Mill's answer to this question, it must be admitted, is profoundly unsatisfactory. 'I regard utility', he says in one place, 'as the ultimate appeal on all ethical questions; but it must be utility in the largest sense, grounded on the permanent interests of man as a progressive being.'[2] Had he gone on to expand this statement by working out a positive theory of these permanent interests, he might have made a real con-tribution to ethics, combining the clarity of the older utilitarians with his own more enlightened views about personality. But he does not do this. All his statements on the subject are in the nature of protests against current miscon-ceptions; all of them include a good many overstatements; and it is singularly unfortunate that in battling against what he regarded as the central misconception of the nineteenth century, Mill should so far have overreached himself as to deny the only source from which it seems possible to fill the empty vessel of individuality.

It was at this time, as Mill describes the situation, that the blight of middle-class respectability was descending upon England. Everyone, from the highest to the lowest class of society, lived 'as under the eye of a hostile and dreaded censorship'; conformity was the first thing thought of; they

---

[1] Morley, *Fortnightly Review,* vol. xvi (1874), p. 648 (condensed).
[2] *Liberty,* chap. i, p. 24.

liked in crowds; they exercised choice only among things commonly done; and the consequence was that the standards in every branch of human endeavour were being more and more firmly set by 'collective mediocrity'. But what then was the remedy? In Mill's opinion it was very simple; as the root of the trouble appeared to him to be the 'despotism of custom', the remedy, he thought, could only be found in a deliberate determination to revolt against custom; consequently he set himself to inculcate the virtue of eccentricity.

In this age [he says], the mere example of non-conformity, the mere refusal to bend the knee to custom, is itself a service. Precisely because the tyranny of opinion is such as to make eccentricity a reproach, it is desirable, in order to break through that tyranny, that people should be eccentric. Eccentricity has always abounded when and where strength of character have abounded; and the amount of eccentricity in a society has generally been proportional to the amount of genius, mental vigour and moral courage which it contains.[1]

But this is simply to substitute one error for another—bohemian nonsense for bourgeois nonsense. Whatever the capacities of any man, in any walk of life, he will necessarily spend a large part of this time in assimilating the traditions of his calling. After that he is usually engaged in a perpetual struggle to be equal to them. It is this which provides the content of his individuality. The assumption of the sort of self-sufficiency that Mill recommends will prevent him from attaining any individuality at all. Nor is the case any different, I believe, with regard to his individuality as a man. Here, again, it is a matter, in the first instance at least, of assimilating the tradition of humanity embodied in the institutions and records of the community in which he is brought up. Although this tradition is always open to correction, it is

[1] Ibid., chap. 3, pp. 110, 118 ff. In Macaulay's opinion, on the other hand, Mill was 'crying fire! in Noah's flood'; and after all it was the age of Dickens and Carlyle, Lear and Browning.

wrong to suggest, as Mill so frequently does, that the finer spirits of the community must be continually at odds with it on all points. There has never yet been a proposal for the reform of morals so extensive that it did not incorporate some elements of the existing scheme. It is always a matter of working within it, pointing to inconsistencies between its various elements and arguing that if we really believe in this, then we must get rid of that. Hence I believe that it is much more realistic to speak in terms of the development of a moral tradition among men than in terms of the development of the men themselves. No doubt the development of the tradition would be impossible without the development of the men. But while the tradition is something that we can usefully talk about, we can only be wise about the potentialities of the men after the event.

12. It would appear, then, that Mill's principle of individuality is not so much a single principle as a bundle of principles of very unequal value:

(i) In its widest and most valuable meaning, this principle may be regarded as asserting that all men should be respected as ends in themselves. Understood in this sense we may say then, as Mill sometimes says, that individuality is synonymous with self-development, where self-development is regarded as involving a sustained attempt to secure 'the conformity of our character to ideal perfection according to some particular standard'.[1] So understood the principle of individuality enabled Mill to correct many of the deficiencies of his predecessors. But this formula, it is to be noted, provides no information about the standard to be adopted.

(ii) If, therefore, the notion of individuality is to be presented as a complete guide to conduct, some content has to be found for it; and this is sometimes done by taking advantage of a completely different meaning of self-development, which stresses the necessity of developing all the

[1] *Logic*, vi. 11. 6. First and second editions only.

potentialities of men. Mill enters an emphatic protest against the adoption of this theory of individuality. Nevertheless his language sometimes seems to imply that he has not completely freed himself from its influence. Consequently, for all the high seriousness with which he expounds it, Mill's doctrine of individuality is apt at times to assume a somewhat frivolous appearance.

(iii) Nor can Mill be absolved from the error of assuming that a man is only himself when he succeeds in being different from other men, as if individuality meant peculiarity or idiosyncrasy. Hence—and this is the greatest weakness in his position—he is led to ignore the fundamental part played by tradition in providing a content for the empty form of individuality.

13. It is, then, easy enough to contrast the muddiness of Mill's ethical ideas with the clarity of those of the older utilitarians. But if there was confusion in his thinking, there was a good deal of humbug in theirs. Their clarity often ends on the pages of their books. They are so desperately anxious to get at the root of the matter, once and for all, that they often disregard the facts that fail to bear them out. They never, as a matter of fact, manage to apply their principles in the rigorous manner they promise. For all the woolliness of Mill's notion of individuality, on the other hand, it is certain that part at least of what he had in mind is both real and important. He failed, it must be admitted, to develop it into a coherent system of ethics; and his attempt to graft it on to the system of utility ended, as perhaps it need not have ended, in utter confusion. But for all that it enabled Mill to analyse the politics of the nineteenth century at a depth that was far beyond the capacity of Bentham.

The principle of individuality provides Mill with a strong argument, supplementary to that of his father, for the widest possible extension of representative government, since he holds that participation in democratic institutions alone can provide the education necessary for the full development of individuality. But the same principle also leads him to be extremely apprehensive of the actions that democratic states may take in the interests of the majority. Hence he is led to suggest safeguards against 'the tyranny of the majority' with which his father would have had, and his father's friends actually had, little sympathy. A similar ambivalent attitude, springing from the same source, is also discernible in his treatment of socialism. On the one hand, he holds that co-operation in industry provides far greater scope for the development of individuality than the wage relation. On the other hand, he is even more suspicious of the state as an employer than of the private capitalist; consequently he considers that it is necessary to retain the institution of private property (with some limitations regarding property in land) as 'a bulwark of human liberty and spontaneity'.[1]

Thus at the end, if we take one essay with another, Mill manages to look at democracy, and even at social democracy, from a good many different points of view; and this indeed constitutes his great strength as a political theorist. He is one of the few men who have had a really substantial idea of democracy (such as he attributed to Tocqueville) as 'something which being a reality in nature and no mere mathematical or metaphysical abstraction manifests itself by innumerable properties'. Moreover the properties of democracy on which he concentrated at the beginning of the nineteenth century are those which have actually turned out to be crucial in the twentieth. He failed, it is true, to solve our difficulties for us, but it can at least be claimed that he foresaw them. The fundamental weakness in his political theory is that he could never make up his mind (any more

[1] Lord Lindsay remarks of Mill that he combines 'an enthusiastic belief in democratic government with most pessimistic apprehensions as to what democracy is likely to do'; and practically everything that is really distinctive in Mill's political thinking seems to be included in this formula.

than we can) upon what terms liberty is to be reconciled with equality, where liberty is that which of all things he most fervently desired and equality is the condition towards which he correctly conceived society to be irresistibly tending.

III

PROS AND CONS OF DEMOCRACY

1. MILL distinguishes three periods in his life. The first was devoted to education and youthful Benthamite propaganda and ends with his breakdown in 1826–7. In the second the influences of 'the reaction of the nineteenth century against the eighteenth' streamed in upon him from France and from Germany, from Coleridge and from Carlyle. They did not on the whole, he thought, induce him to ignore 'that half of the truth which the eighteenth century saw'; the fight between the eighteenth and nineteenth centuries reminded him rather of the battle about the shield, one side of which was white and the other black; and Goethe's device, 'Many-sidedness', was one which he would most willingly have taken for his own at this period.

Nevertheless he gradually became aware that the impetus with which he had detached himself 'from whatever was untenable in the doctrines of Bentham and of the eighteenth century' had perhaps carried him too far in the opposite direction. Consequently in the third period he 'completely turned back from what there had been of excess' in his reaction against Benthamism. Indeed he considered that at this time his opinions were 'far *more* heretical' than they had been in the days of his most extreme Benthamism. 'We were now', he says, speaking also for his wife, 'much less democrats than I had been, because so long as education continued to be so wretchedly imperfect, we dreaded the ignorance and especially the selfishness and brutality of the mass; but our ideal of ultimate improvement went far beyond Democracy and would class us decidedly under the general designation of Socialists.'

Thus if we disregard what Mill has to say in the first period of his life where he merely repeats the teaching of Bentham, it would seem that his political theories comprise two rather different sets of doctrines; and it was during the publication of the various editions of his *Political Economy* and under the influence of the European revolutions of 1848, as he tells us, that he made the transition from the first set to the second.

In the first edition [he says], the difficulties of socialism were stated so strongly that the tone was on the whole that of opposition to it. In the year or two which followed, much time was given to the study of the best socialistic writers on the continent; and the result was that most of what had been written on the subject in the first edition was cancelled, and replaced by arguments and reflections which represent a more advanced opinion.[1]

2. When, however, we find how Mill interprets these statements, they turn out to mean considerably less than we might expect. Mill considered himself a socialist, it appears, because he 'looked forward' to a time when society would no longer be divided between the idle and the industrious and when the division of the produce of labour would be made on acknowledged principles of justice. But at the same time he disclaimed any knowledge of the 'precise form of institutions' by which these objects could most effectively be obtained. He was clear enough that the doctrine of his essay on *Liberty* was 'diametrically opposite' to some of the projects of socialists, since it recognized 'no authority whatever in society over the individual, except to enforce [*sic*] equal freedom of development for all individuals'; and his theory of property also told in the same direction.[2]

Thus it is impossible to accept at its face value Mill's statement regarding the predominantly socialist trend of his political thinking in the third period of his life. Indeed if it is examined at all closely, it is plainly an incredible statement. He was, he says, less of a democrat than he had been because

---

[1] *Autobiography*, pp. 136 ff.; 194 ff.; 198.
[2] Ibid., pp. 196 ff.; 214 ff.

he dreaded the ignorance and brutality of the mass *and yet* his ideal of ultimate improvement went far beyond democracy in the direction of socialism. Did he, then, consider the ignorance and brutality of the mass to be less of an obstacle to socialism than to democracy? The fact is that during his third period Mill's political thinking developed along two quite different and inconsistent lines. On the one hand, advocating a sort of homoeopathic cure for the ills of democracy, he became more of a democrat and, in the process, a bit of a socialist. On the other hand, convinced of 'the tendency of democracy towards bearing down individuality and circumscribing the exercise of the human faculties', he became less of a democrat and attempted to lay down limits (along the lines of the social contract theorists) beyond which governmental interference with the individual should never go.

Thus, correcting the account that Mill gives us of the development of his political theory after he had begun to think for himself, I would suggest that it comprises three and not merely two sets of doctrine. There is first the doctrine of his middle period when he was under the influence of Coleridge; secondly, the doctrine of his later period when, reacting sharply against conservatism, he became more democratic and slightly socialistic; thirdly, the concurrent doctrine of his later period in which he was concerned above all to protect the individual from the tyranny of the majority. Fortunately, however, there are connecting links between these different sets of doctrine, and one in particular promises to be of considerable help in understanding the relations between them. Whenever he discusses politics Mill always makes some reference to his father's *Essay on Government*. This, therefore, may be regarded as a sort of hinge or pivot on which his political thinking turns.

3. In James Mill's eyes, we have seen, the best form of government is that which provides the greatest security

against the governing body's abuse of its power; and granted his assumption that everybody pursues his own interest at the expense of everybody else, it follows that the representative system is the best. It also follows that the government should be elected by a universal franchise, since otherwise it will inevitably abuse its power over those who, having no votes, have no power over it; and although this was not, as a matter of fact, the conclusion drawn by James Mill[1] it was perfectly plain to all those concerned in the debate over parliamentary reform that it ought to have been.

Even when James Mill's position is thus corrected, however, it is still open to a fundamental objection. Although the representative system ensures that the government cannot persistently act in opposition to what the people regard as their interest, it provides, and can provide, no guarantee that they will form a correct idea of their interest. It is in pursuance of this objection that Macaulay predicts, in one of the most famous of his purple passages, that the acceptance of the radical case for parliamentary reform, with its inevitable corollary of universal enfranchisement, can only end in a deluge of barbarism;[2] and James Mill's reply to this objection exposes with unexpected ingenuousness the essentially middle-class outlook of the older utilitarians.

Completely abandoning all his old principles he lays it down first, that the middle rank is 'both the most wise and the most virtuous part of the community'; secondly, that 'the opinions of that class of the people who are below the middle

[1] He held that the right to vote might 'without inconvenience' be restricted to men and even to men over forty. *Essay on Government* (Cambridge), pp. 35, 45 ff.

[2] Macaulay, *Miscellaneous Writings* (1860), i. 314. 'Is it possible', asks Macaulay, 'that in two or three hundred years, a few lean and half naked fishermen may divide with owls and foxes the ruins of the greatest European cities, may wash their nets amidst the relics of her gigantic docks and build their huts out of the capitals of her stately cathedrals?' He answers that if we accept the principles of Mr. Mill it is possible.

rank are formed, and their minds are directed by that intelligent and virtuous rank'. Hence he arrives at the astonishing conclusion that it simply does not matter in the long run who elects the members of the government, since in any case the middle rank is 'that portion of the community of which, if the basis of representation were ever so far extended, the opinion would ultimately decide'.[1]

4. Thus in practice the Whig, Macaulay, and the Radical, James Mill, entertained surprisingly similar expectations regarding parliamentary reform. Macaulay understood the principle of the Reform Bill to be the admission of 'the middle rank to a large and direct share in the representation without any violent shock to the institutions' of the country. Consequently he supported the proposal both because it would improve those institutions and, more particularly, because it would preserve them—because, in short, it provided the 'best security against revolution'. While then, the logical outcome of James Mill's argument for reform was universal suffrage, Macaulay supported reform precisely in order to avoid universal suffrage; and no opposition, it would seem, could be more absolute. But in fact James Mill only supported an extension of the suffrage in the belief that the working class would always follow the lead of the middle class; and Macaulay is simply stating the plain truth when he remarks that 'the system of universal suffrage according to Mr. Mill's own account is only a device for doing circuitously what a representative system with a pretty high qualification would do directly'.[2]

---

[1] James Mill, op. cit., pp. 71 ff.

[2] Macaulay, op. cit., p. 316. There is no foundation at all for Halévy's suggestion (*Growth of Philosophical Radicalism*, pp. 421–6) that Macaulay endorsed the radical argument for reform in his parliamentary speeches. His argument is, in fact, the direct contrary to theirs. 'That we may exclude those whom it is necessary to exclude', he maintained, 'we must admit those whom it is safe to admit.' *Speech on Parliamentary Reform*, 2/3/31.

J. S. Mill, however, was unable to share his father's naïve belief that the labouring classes would always regard their interests as identical with those of their employers. He was convinced, moreover, that it would not be a good thing if they did. Thus failing to find in the predominance of the middle class any guarantee, such as his father found, that a representative government, elected by an extensive franchise, would act in the best interests of the people, Mill was driven to the conclusion that his father's doctrine contained only part of the truth about politics; and all his subsequent thinking on the subject may be regarded as a search for means to supplement it.

Conservative Doctrine of the Early Essays

5. In his middle period when he was most under the influence of the nineteenth-century reaction against the eighteenth century, Mill lays it down that there are three great questions concerning government; and he criticizes Bentham and his father on the ground that they applied themselves exclusively to the third question and hence inevitably prejudiced any tenable answer to the other two questions. These three questions are: (i) To what authority is it for the good of the people that they should be subject? (ii) How are they to be induced to obey that authority? (iii) By what means are the abuses of this authority to be checked?

European reformers [says Mill] have been accustomed to see the numerical majority everywhere unjustly depressed; everywhere trampled upon or at the best overlooked by governments; nowhere possessing power enough to extort redress of their most positive grievances. To see these things and to seek to put an end to them by means (among other things) of giving more political power to the majority, constitutes Radicalism; and it is because so many in this age have felt this wish that such a theory of government as Bentham's has found favour with them.

But the numerical majority of any society, Mill argues, must consist of persons all standing in the same social position and having in the main the same pursuits. 'Where there is identity of position and pursuits, there will also be identity of partialities, passions and prejudices.' To give absolute power to the numerical majority is, therefore, to make 'one narrow, mean type of human nature universal and perpetual, and to crush every influence which tends to the further improvement of man's intellectual nature'. Hence Mill maintained that the radicals were not making the best use of their powers when they 'exhausted all the resources of ingenuity in devising means for riveting the yoke of public opinion closer and closer round the necks of functionaries'. Moreover while he admitted that there must be some paramount power in society and that it was on the whole right that the majority should be that power, he insisted that the institutions of society should also make provision for keeping up 'a perpetual and standing opposition to the will of the majority', by the establishment of some sort of aristocracy.[1]

'The idea of a rational democracy', he says, 'is not that the people themselves govern but that they have security for good government. The people ought to be the masters, but they are masters who must employ servants more skilful than themselves; like a ministry when they employ a military commander, or the military commander when he employs an army surgeon.' Thus he rejects the view that the many should evoke all political questions to their own tribunal and decide them according to their own judgement. This course would, he admits, compel philosophers 'to enlighten the multitude and render them capable of appreciating their more profound views'. But while he would attach great value to this consequence of popular government, if it were capable of being realized, he does not think at this period of his life that it is. 'How', he asks, 'will philosophers bring these truths home to

[1] *Dissertations*, i. 378–82.

the perception of the multitude? Can they enable common sense to judge of science, or inexperience of experience?' Hence for his part he prefers to rely on 'the deliberately formed opinions of a comparatively few specially educated for the task', like the aristocracies of experienced and laborious men who had governed Rome, Venice, and Holland, and continued to govern Prussia and British India.[1]

6. It is true that when Mill comes to make concrete suggestions regarding the way in which government by the wise is to be combined with control by the people, he becomes vague and uncertain. In one of his early essays he suggests that the solution is to be found in the encouragement of 'an agricultural class, a leisured class, and a learned class' to counterbalance the commercial middle class. In another, he proposes to breathe new life into a second chamber by appointing to it 'persons no longer young whose reputation is already gained'.[2] But although the bias of his mind is sufficiently evident, he can scarcely be said to have given any very explicit answer to what he regards as the first question of government: to what authority is it for the good of the people that they should be subject?

He is, however, considerably more explicit regarding the answer to be given to the second question: how are the people to be induced to obey that authority? Here indeed he reaches the high-water mark of his reaction against Bentham and the philosophers of the eighteenth century. Their error, he thought, was not, as was commonly alleged, that they trusted too little to the moral feelings of men but rather that they trusted to them too much. 'They thought them the natural and spontaneous growth of the human heart; so firmly fixed in it, that they would subsist unimpaired, nay invigorated, when the whole system of opinions and observances with which they were habitually intertwined was violently torn away.' Hence it was in this state of mind that they set to work to

---

[1] Ibid. i. 467–74.   [2] Ibid. ii. 73; 82.

annihilate superstition and priestcraft, never for one moment suspecting that 'when the noxious weeds were once rooted out, the soil would stand in any need of tillage'.

In Mill's opinion, however, obedience to a government was not such an easy thing to establish in this world that it should be so lightly jeopardized; and he endeavours to counteract the influence of the root-and-branch men of the eighteenth century by enumerating certain conditions which are essential to a stable society. Thus he points to the fact that all states have found it essential to submit their citizens to a system of education 'of which one main and necessary ingredient was *restraining discipline*'. It is also, he maintains, a condition of permanent political society that there should exist among all its members a feeling of allegiance or loyalty to the state; and this, in Mill's opinion at this time, requires them to assume that there is in its constitution '*something* which is settled, something permanent and not to be called in question whatever else may change'—'*something* which has in the common estimation been placed beyond discussion'.[1]

It was at this last remark of Mill's that the orthodox utilitarians began to be seriously alarmed about him. Grote regarded it as nothing but 'an expression of the standing intolerance of society towards unpopular opinions' and his admiration for Mill was always subsequently to be tinged with fear, because he never knew what unexpected turn Mill might take. Mrs. Grote acquired the habit of referring to him now as 'the lama', now as 'that wayward intellectual deity'. Francis Place commented with all the unction of a man beyond the reach of temptation—'I think John Mill has made great progress in becoming a German metaphysician. Eccentricity and obscurity must necessarily be the result.'[2] If, however, Grote and his friends had been able to foresee the

---

[1] *Dissertations*, i. 414–21; *Logic*, vi. 10. 5.
[2] Bain, *J. S. Mill*, pp. 57; 83. Graham Wallas, *Francis Place*, p. 91 and footnote.

changes that the next few years would bring, they might have found grounds for comfort; for Mill was now to be animated by the strongest repugnance to the counter-revolutionary sympathies that had influenced him here.

7. Nor is this change in Mill's opinions to be attributed entirely to inconstancy on his part, since the changing times had introduced a new note into counter-revolutionary propaganda. Instead of Coleridge it was now Carlyle who reigned supreme; and in spite of a brief flirtation with Carlyle's beliefs, Mill was not long in deciding that nothing could be made of them. As some men are born to rule and others to obey, Carlyle considered that there was only one fundamental problem in politics—that of persuading the right men to rule and the rest to obey. Hence the twofold burden of all his political writings. On the one hand, the lower classes are reminded that 'obedience is the primary duty of man'. On the other hand, the upper classes are warned that, one way or another, this world will absolutely need to be governed; if not by this class of men, then by that. A *real* aristocracy, then, has to be found; an apparent one was of no more use to England than it had been to France before the Revolution.

As the tide of liberalism grew in Europe, Carlyle's references to the French Revolution become correspondingly more fevered. In 1843 he describes it as 'the Cruellest Portent that has risen into Created Space these ten centuries'. Six years later, after the revolutions of 1848, he translates it into a terrifying vision of the 'enlightened public' rushing towards the Sea of Tiberius and the bottomless cloacas of nature like one huge Gadarene's Swinery. But apart from the increasing vividness with which he points to the alternatives to a real government by a *real* aristocracy, the theme is always the same. It is the underlying theme also of Newman's lifelong antipathy to liberalism. It has never been better summarized than in an aphorism of Disraeli's—'Man is made to adore and obey; but if you will not command him, if you give him nothing to worship, he will fashion his own divinities and find a chieftain in his own passions.'

It was in these circumstances—fired, on the one hand, by the European revolutions of 1848 and disgusted, on the other, by the utterances of those who opposed them—that Mill set his face against the conservative influences that had previously weighed so heavily with him. 'Instead of reverent discipleship which he aspired to', as Carlyle put it, 'Mill now seems to have taken the function of getting up to contradict whatever I say.' And so indeed, or vice versa, it was to appear throughout the early-Victorian period. Between them, Mill and Carlyle were generally regarded as defining from opposite sides all the principal social issues of the time and so far, at least, as one section of Mill's writings is concerned, this view is substantially correct.

The Case for Democracy and Co-operation

8. Mill's most explicit statement regarding the central social issue of the nineteenth century occurs in his *Political Economy* where, after remarking on 'the existence of two conflicting theories respecting the social position desirable for manual labourers', he defends the theory of what he calls self-dependence against the opposite theory of dependence or protection.[1] According to the latter, as he understands it, 'The lot of the poor in all things which affect them collectively should be regulated *for* them, not *by* them.' Thus it is supposed to be the duty of the higher classes to think for the lower as

---

[1] The sort of sentiments that Mill has in mind as constituting the core of the Victorian counter-revolutionary position are those expressed by one of Dickens's characters. 'What man can do *I* do', says Sir Joseph Bowley in *The Chimes*. 'I do my duty as the Poor Man's Friend and Father, and I endeavour to educate his mind by inculcating on all occasions the one great moral lesson which that class requires. That is, entire Dependence on Myself. They have no business whatever with—with themselves.' It is, perhaps, with some recollection of this passage that Mill, who was an inveterate reader of Dickens, calls this theory that of dependence or protection and asserts in opposition to it his own theory of self-dependence.

officers do for their soldiers and parents for their children; men, it is also said, should stand in the same relation to women; and as the idea of a society held together only by pecuniary interests is 'essentially repulsive', so Mill is prepared to concede that there is something naturally attractive in this picture of a society abounding in strong personal attachments and disinterested devotion. Nevertheless he is emphatic that the theory of dependence has to be rejected and he offers two arguments against it, one derived from his father and the other peculiarly his own.

In the first place, although the exponents of this theory are constantly appealing to history, Mill agrees with his father that they give a completely false account of it so far as the behaviour of the privileged classes is concerned. With the exception of an individual here and there, Mill holds, they have always used their power in their own interests and not in caring for the unprivileged; and, although he would not deny that the selfish feelings engendered by power might be corrected, he was convinced 'that long before the superior classes could be sufficiently improved to govern in the tutelary manner supposed, the inferior classes would be too much improved to be so governed'. In the second place, Mill considered that the inferior classes were already too much improved to be governed in this manner. They had already taken their interests into their own hands and were perpetually showing that they thought them not identical with but opposite to those of their employers. 'Hence we have now to learn', he concludes, 'that the well-being of a people exists by means of precisely those qualities which the theory of dependence attempts to dispense with—the justice and self-government of the individual citizens.'[1]

Stating the same position rather more elaborately, Mill holds that a form of government affects the welfare of the government in two different ways: first, as an arrangement

[1] *Political Economy*, iv. 7. 1 and 2.

for conducting the collective affairs of the community; secondly, as an agency of national education. Hence he argues that there are two criteria of any form of government: first, the degree to which it takes advantage of the existing good qualities of the citizens in conducting public affairs; secondly, the degree to which it increases them; and judging by either criterion he concludes that the best form of government is that in which the supreme controlling power is vested in the entire aggregate of the community and every citizen is occasionally called on to take an actual part in the government, by the personal discharge of some public function.

It is not sufficiently considered [he says] how little there is in most men's ordinary lives to give any largeness either to their conceptions or to their sentiments. Giving him something to do for the public supplies, in a measure, these deficiencies. If circumstances allow the amount of public duty assigned to him to be considerable, it makes him an educated man.

As evidence of this he points to the high intellectual standard reached by the average Athenian citizen.[1]

9. Thus while Mill's case for representative government, at this period, may still be said to rest, like his father's, on a regard for the interests of the governed, he had a profoundly different idea of what constitutes their interests. James Mill took it for granted not only that everybody pursues his own interests but also that his interests are given with him and are not susceptible to change. Hence he readily came to the conclusion that a government was only to be trusted when it could be turned out of office by the governed whose interests it neglected. But it never occurred to him to call upon the governed to moderate their demands, in their own interests, by the exercise of justice and self-government. Any such suggestion he would have regarded as Utopian and as prompted, most probably, by some sinister interest. More-

---

[1] *Representative Government*, chaps. 2 and 3.

over J. S. Mill widened as well as deepened the utilitarian position. The older generation had not seriously envisaged the possibility, or perhaps even the desirability, of extending the franchise beyond the middle classes to whom it was actually granted by the Reform Bill of 1832. James Mill, at least, was opposed to extending it to women. In both these respects J. S. Mill was considerably more radical and rigorous than his father; and in another respect he breaks completely new ground by applying the doctrine of self-dependence beyond the constitutional to the industrial sphere.

The idea of industrial co-operation was, indeed, so much in the air at this time that even Carlyle had once glanced briefly at it. As one might expect, however, he had immediately and finally dismissed the suggestion on the ground that 'despotism is essential in most enterprises'. Ruskin, again, who generally followed Carlyle very closely in his utterances about social affairs, thought that co-operation was perhaps not expedient, because there is a root of 'the very deepest and holiest truth' in the saying about 'the duty of remaining content in the position in which Providence has placed you'.[1]

For Mill, however, the co-operative idea seemed to offer the only possible permanent solution of the industrial question. He did not think that the labouring classes would be permanently content to work for wages; but except in the newer countries they had few opportunities of becoming employers; and in any case, he contends, the wage relation is nearly as unsatisfactory to the employer as to the employee. Hence Mill considered that the form of industrial association to which we must look forward, 'if mankind continues to improve', is that of labourers who collectively own the capital with which they carry on their operations and work under managers elected and removable by themselves. Co-operation, he argues, has a great material advantage in the vast stimulus

[1] Carlyle, *Past and Present* (Popular Edition), pp. 421 f.; Ruskin, *Time and Tide*, Letter 2.

that production will receive when it is to the interests of the workers to do their utmost instead of the least possible, but its real importance lay rather in the moral revolution that it would bring about. In Mill's opinion it would convert 'each human being's daily occupation into a school of the social sympathies and the practical intelligence', and finally transform 'human life from a conflict of classes struggling for opposite interests to a friendly rivalry in the pursuit of a good common to all'.[1]

10. Nevertheless Mill does not lose sight during this period of the dangers and infirmities of democracy with which he had been so concerned earlier; and in an endeavour to combat them he suggests several sets of safeguards, some of which are consistent with his advanced democratic views and others which are not. Thus he argues that there is a radical distinction between controlling the business of government and actually doing it. No progress at all, he thinks, can be made towards attaining a skilled democracy unless the democracy is willing that the work which requires skill should be left to those who possess it. Hence he strongly recommends the development of a permanent and highly trained civil service with fairly wide powers; and since he is here on ground with which he is thoroughly familiar, what he has to say regarding both the strength and the weaknesses of bureaucracy is still very worth-while reading.[2]

Then, again, he recommends the adoption of a number of electoral devices (public voting, plural voting on an educational basis and proportional representation) which he considers will secure the return to parliament of men of higher calibre than had previously been elected. But his attitude here is much less realistic and his devices, when they have been tried, have not worn at all well. It was in connexion with his advocacy of public voting that Bright let fall the acid remark,

---

[1] *Political Economy*, iv. 7. 4 and 6.
[2] *Representative Government*, chap. 5.

'The worst of great thinkers is that they so often think wrong';
and Disraeli's characterization of Mill as 'the finishing
governess' is more applicable to this part of his work than to
any other.[1]

These safeguards, moreover, even if they were workable,
deal with only half the problem as Mill sees it. There were,
he thought, two main dangers to be apprehended from the
development of democracy: first, the danger of a low grade
of intelligence in the representative body such as, according
to Tocqueville, commonly obtained among the representative bodies of America; secondly, the danger of class legislation and of other forms of social pressure in the interest of
the numerical majority; and while the institution of a civil
service with pretty wide powers, along with the adoption of
Mill's electoral devices, might cope adequately with the
former danger, they would have little effect against the latter.
Thus Mill also considered that it was necessary to institute a
more sweeping safeguard against what he regarded as the
more dangerous infirmity of democracy. He suggests here,
in that part of his political theory which is peculiarly characteristic of him, that we should endeavour to insulate the
individual against the deforming pressures of society by means
of a sort of pact of non-interference, which is to be based
upon a theory of the social union quite remote from any
doctrine of his that has so far been considered and even more
remote from any doctrine of Bentham's.

---

[1] Ibid., chaps. 7 and 8. In dealing both with proportional representation
and with plural, or rather with multiple, voting Mill betrays a most
melancholy preoccupation with arithmetic. The assumptions on which his
computations are based in the two cases are, moreover, mutually contradictory. The argument by which he supports proportional representation
is that it would ensure, as a really equal democracy should, that every
section of the community is represented according to its numerical
strength. In regard to multiple voting, on the contrary, Mill proposes
that while every person should have at least one vote, the better educated
should have more than one, 'on a scale corresponding as far as practicable
to their amount of education'. *Dissertations*, iii. 21 f.

The Argument for Insulation

11. On the whole, and particularly in the sphere of economics, Bentham believed in letting people alone to pursue their interests in their own way, because he held that they were then most likely to promote the general interest. Nevertheless he was quite clear that the power of government, 'though not *infinite* must unavoidably be allowed to be *indefinite*' except in the very special case where the power of a federal government is limited by the powers of its constituent states. Hence, with this exception, he regarded it 'as an abuse of language' to say of any government that 'there is any act they *cannot* do' or 'to speak of their exceeding their authority'; and it is plain that any other conclusion would have been inconsistent with his position, since the only ground which he has for objecting to governmental interference is simply that of inutility.[1]

For Mill, however, the case is utterly different. As the end of life is self-development, the prime duty of government for him is to assist self-development. Hence he is led to a double disagreement with Bentham. On the one hand he asserts the propriety of some sorts of governmental interference in the interests of the subject which Bentham would have wholeheartedly opposed. (Thus he supports the state provision, but not the state monopoly, of elementary education; and thus he also supports factory legislation on behalf of children though not of adults.) On the other hand, and here he departs even further from orthodoxy, he asserts the absolute impropriety of other sorts of interference and, in fact, talks in precisely the way that Bentham condemns as an abuse of language.

Such phrases as 'self-government' and 'the power of the people over themselves', he now argues, cannot be regarded as describing the state of affairs that had arisen, or was likely to arise, in any state. The people who exercise the power are

---

[1] Bentham, *Fragment on Government*, chap. 4, paras. 23, 26.

not the same as those over whom it is exercised and the self-government spoken of is not the government of each by himself but of each by all the rest. 'The people, consequently, *may* desire to oppress a part of their number; and precautions are as much needed against this as against any other abuse of power.' Unlike other tyrannies, moreover, the tyranny of the majority does not operate only through the acts of public authority. 'Society can and does execute its own mandates'; and thereby it practises a social tyranny more formidable than many kinds of political oppression since, though not upheld by such extreme penalties, it leaves fewer means of escape, penetrates more deeply into the details of life, and enslaves the soul itself. 'Protection, therefore, against the tyranny of the magistrate is not enough: there needs protection also against the tyranny of prevailing opinion and feeling which would compel all other characters to fashion themselves upon the model of its own.'[1]

But where is such protection to be found? By this time Mill is convinced that it cannot be found in any device of government and so he turns instead to a proposal for limiting the power of government. 'Whatever thing we adopt respecting the foundation of the social union', he now says, 'and under whatever political institutions we live, there is a circle around every individual human being which no government, be it that of one, of a few, or of the many, ought to be permitted to overstep.' Moreover while he admits that there may be some difference of opinion regarding the area which should thus be 'sacred from authoritarian intrusion', he is prepared to define it with considerable precision. 'The only part of the conduct of anybody, for which he is amenable to society', he maintains, 'is that which concerns others. In the part which merely concerns himself his independence is of right absolute. Over himself, over his own body and mind, the individual is sovereign.'[2]

---

[1] *Liberty*, chap. 1, pp. 12 f.
[2] *Political Economy*, v. 11. 2; *Liberty*, chap. 1, p. 22.

12. It is strange that Mill, who usually had an extremely keen eye for any sort of moral unhealthiness, should have failed to detect the taint of corruption here. One can only suppose that he was blind to the temptations offered by this doctrine because he was immune to them himself. But however that may be, it seems perfectly plain that it is a completely untenable as well as a completely impracticable doctrine. It is quite impossible to distinguish between that part of a person's behaviour which affects himself and that part which also affects others; and there is nothing to be gained by attempting to make the distinction. It is necessary, says Mill, to provide an area within which individuality may be freely developed; but the only sort of individuality that is likely to be developed under these circumstances is the sort that is utterly worthless —the hothouse individuality of caprice and pretence.

The danger here may be illustrated from Mill's answer to a question raised at the beginning of his chapter on the liberty of thought and discussion. He asks: is it legitimate to advocate the doctrine of tyrannicide? He answers, as he is bound to answer (since he must distinguish between that part of a man's conduct which only affects himself and that part which also affects others), that there ought to exist the fullest liberty of professing and discussing this doctrine 'as a matter of ethical conviction'; but that the instigation to it, in a specific case, may be a proper subject of punishment, if an overt act has followed as a consequence.[1]

But what, in fact, does this answer amount to? The assump-

---

[1] *Liberty*, chap. 2, footnote at beginning. Mill also gives a similar decision a little later. 'An opinion', he says, 'that corn dealers are starvers of the poor, or that private property is robbery ought to be unmolested when *simply circulated* through the press but may justly incur punishment when delivered orally to an excited mob assembled before the house of a corn dealer, or when handed out among the same mob in the form of a placard' (ibid., chap. 3 at beginning; my italics). How can you possibly be sure that an opinion will *simply circulate* through the press, without affecting anybody's action? If you can be sure of this, why should you bother to express an opinion?

tion upon which it is based is that a principle may be held in general—as a matter of ethical conviction—along with the complete absence of any intention to apply it in particular cases and even with the fully formed intention never to apply it. The obvious comment is that a man who holds a principle in this sort of way does not hold it at all but merely pretends to hold it; and the case of the man who, professing a doctrine which he is not prepared to apply, induces others to apply it, is a good deal worse. No man, it would usually, and, in my opinion, correctly be said, has any right to profess the doctrine of tyrannicide unless he is prepared to do his share of tyrant-killing. Still less has he any right to persuade others to adopt that doctrine unless he is prepared to take full responsibility for any tyrants who may thereby be killed, even at second or third hand. In practice, moreover, it will be extremely difficult to distinguish between a personal profession of tyrannicide and an attempt at persuasion.

13. I do not suggest that all the cases discussed by Mill in the essay on *Liberty* lead to such extreme difficulties as this. It is, I think, true that in the great majority of them it is best, from the point of view equally of the individual and of society, to let people alone to do as they think right. At any rate the onus, it may safely be said, is always on the other party to prove the contrary. Hence Mill's general argument for the toleration of heterodox opinion is, I believe, perfectly sound. —'If the opinion is right,' he says, 'men are deprived of the opportunity of exchanging error for truth; if wrong, they lose what is almost as great a benefit, the clear perception and livelier impression of truth produced by its collision with error.'[1]

But all the same there are several points to be noted about this argument if it is not to be misapplied. First, it has no connexion at all with the argument for insulation to which the essay on *Liberty* is ostensibly devoted. It does not lead to the

---

[1] Ibid., p. 33.

conclusion that men should be separated from each other like so many windowless monads. On the contrary, it rests on the assumption that there is to be the freest interchange of opinions among men. It is an argument for interaction rather than insulation.

Secondly, its recognition as a sound general argument for the free expression of heterodox opinion is by no means incompatible with the admission that in some subjects, in some circumstances, there may be stronger arguments against the expression of such opinions. No doubt there is danger in admitting exceptions of this sort since they may so easily be used as precedents in cases where the circumstances are not similar; but the danger on the other side is, I think, even greater; if you decline to admit exceptions under any circumstances (for example, in time of war) you immediately expose your general rule to a *reductio ad absurdem* from which it will never recover. In this respect, moreover, Mill's treatment of liberty represents a definite retrogression from the standard set by Bentham for the discussion of politics; for, if the utilitarians of the old school had been notable for nothing else, they would still be entitled to a good deal of credit for stressing the fact that most political questions have to be decided by balancing sets of opposing considerations.

Thirdly, Mill persistently ignores one consideration which is extremely relevant here. He assumes that the question of freedom of speech and publication is entirely concerned with 'opinions' which will be judged by all concerned with complete dispassion. But the actual position, of course, is that we have also to do with things that, for some people at least, rank rather as immediate stimuli to action. The case, for example, for the censorship of pornographic literature (which Mill never mentions) is that it immediately incites some people to act in undesirable ways. No doubt it would be better for all concerned if they would dispassionately discuss the 'opinions' implied in such literature. But the fact of the matter is that they will not and pending a radical re-education of the species it would appear that the withdrawal of such literature from general circulation does make for the greatest good of the greatest number. The difficulty is, of course, to define *such* literature seeing that its bad effects depend as much on the reader as on the author.

14. The extent of the inconsistency of Mill's latest line of thought with orthodox utilitarianism and, I would add, of its inferiority to it, also appears very clearly when we compare the theory of property to which it led Mill with the theories professed by Hume and Bentham. Mill's theory of property involves such an extraordinary regression to the sort of theory based on natural rights rather than utility that had been current before the days of Hume and Bentham, that we have to go right back to Locke to find its inspiration. 'Though the earth and all inferior creatures be common to all men', says Locke, 'yet every man has a *property* in his own *person.*' Whatsoever, then, a man removes out of the state that nature has left it in becomes his, quite independently of any laws passed by the community, because 'he hath mixed his own labour with it and joined to it something that is his own'.— 'The institution of property', says Mill, 'when limited to its essential elements, consists in the recognition, in each person, of a right to the exclusive disposal of what he or she have produced by their own exertions'; and he adds that 'the owner's power either of use or of exclusion should be absolute except', and this is the only concession he makes to utility, 'when positive evil would result from it.'[1]

It is true that Mill found himself unable, in Locke's facile fashion, to stretch this doctrine sufficiently far to justify absolute ownership of land, since that is 'not of man's creation but a mere gift of nature'. Thus in regard to land Mill pressed for some restriction of property rights. In particular, he

[1] Locke, *Second Essay concerning Government,* paras. 27 f.; Mill, *Political Economy,* ii. 2 and 6.

initiated a movement to collect from the landlord by taxation as much of his income as had accrued to him, in Mill's phrase, by way of 'unearned increment'. Indeed he regarded this as such an important proposal that in the last years of his life he founded *The Land Tenure Reform Association* to forward it. But in this there was nothing inconsistent with his labour theory of property. On the contrary, the whole point of Mill's proposal is that the landlord has not earned the increment that comes to him by reason of the growth of towns, the extension of manufactures, and so on.

Moreover it is perfectly plain that the recognition of a natural right to property based on labour (which turns out to include the labour of abstinence) must inevitably limit the application of any schemes of socialization based on utility. Indeed this was a substantial part of Mill's case for his land reform proposals. He argued that if the landlords refused to accept his modest proposals, they would inevitably be faced with the more extreme demands of those who believed in the nationalization of land. Hence in this case he was able to represent himself, reasonably enough, as the advocate of a middle course based on the principles of justice which would save the British people from the rising tide of socialist agitation.

Even those [he urges] who take the most unfavourable view of the changes in our social arrangements which are demanded with increasing energy on behalf of the working classes, would be wise to consider that when claims are made which are partly just and partly beyond the limits of justice, it is no less politic than honest to concede with a good will all that is just, and take their defensive stand on the line, if they are able to find it, which separates justice from injustice.[1]

15. Turn now to Hume and Bentham and the case is entirely different. It is requisite for the peace and interest of

---

[1] *Dissertations*, iv. 265. For the programme of the Land Tenure Association see pp. 239 f., footnote.

society, according to Hume, that men's possessions should be separated; and the rules which we follow in making the separation, he holds, are such as can best be contrived to serve further the interests of society. Thus we secure to a man whatever he produces by his art or industry, 'in order to give him encouragement to such useful habits and accomplishments'; we allow him to alienate his property by consent, 'in order to beget that commerce and intercourse which is so beneficial to human society'; we watch carefully over the fulfilment of promises, 'in order to secure mutual trust and confidence, by which the general *interest* of mankind is so much promoted'. But Hume is consistent enough to recognize that the same rule of utility which prescribes a general respect for the rights of property also justifies their occasional violation;[1] and, generally speaking, Bentham follows the same line of thought as Hume, although here again we have to note the devastating influence that the middle-class affiliations of the utilitarians sometimes had upon their logic.

'Property', Bentham lays down, 'is only a foundation of expectation—the expectation of deriving certain advantages from the thing said to be possessed'; and this expectation, he points out, can only be implemented by law; it is, for example, from the law alone that I can enclose a field and give myself to its cultivation in the distant hope of the harvest. Thus property and law are born and must die together. 'Before the laws there was no property: take away the laws, all property ceases.' But although this might seem to presage a claim on behalf of the legislator to dispose as he pleased of the property of the various members of the community in the interest of the greatest good of the greatest number, Bentham's argument actually takes a different turn. It is, he holds, these

[1] 'The safety of the people', he says, 'is the supreme law: all other particular laws are subordinate to it and dependent on it: and if in the *common* cause of things, they be followed and regarded, it is only because the public safety and interest *commonly* demand so equal and impartial an administration.' *Enquiry concerning Morals*, sect. iii, part 2.

expectations in regard to property which alone have overcome man's natural aversion to labour and have bestowed on him the empire of the earth. Hence he argues that the legislator owes the greatest possible respect to these expectations. He even goes so far as to say that when the legislator 'does not interfere with them he does all that is essential to the happiness of society'.[1]

But although, in the turn he gives to it, Bentham's theory of property prescribes the maintenance of the distribution which is actually established, 'whether in America, England, Hungary, or Russia', it is remarkably easy to turn it in the opposite direction and justify on his general principles that interference with property rights which has actually occurred in most countries since his time. Men, says Bentham, can only form plans on the basis of expectations; and we agree. But, he goes on, it is in the general interest that men should be able to form plans; consequently the state should guarantee that some, at least, of their expectations should not be disappointed; and we still agree. Hence, he concludes, the first duty of the legislator is to maintain, as far as possible, the actual distribution of property; and we disagree; not because we believe that expectations in regard to property have no claim to consideration, but because we hold that men have other wants whose satisfaction should also be guaranteed by the legislature.

Men should be secure, we now usually argue, not only from the deprivation of their property, but also from unemployment when they are able and willing to work; from hunger when they are no longer able to work; at all times from remedial ill health. Thus having decided, in the general interest, on the relative importance of these various wants, it is the duty of the government, we hold, to determine which shall be sacrificed and to what extent. It is because we believe that it is as important to satisfy the last of these wants as the first

[1] Bentham, *Principles of the Civil Code*, part 1, chaps. 7–11.

that we have formulated our schemes of social security. But the very name—social security—suggests that in adopting this policy we have not been uninfluenced by Bentham, since security is the general heading under which he discusses all the steps that should be taken by governments to encourage men to build expectations upon the basis of needs.

Conclusion

16. In one sense all Mill's political thinking may be described as an extension of his father's *Essay on Government*, in that he was perpetually concerned with the fact that on his father's premises (which he accepted) there is as inevitable a tendency in democracy towards a tyranny of the majority as there is in monarchy towards a tyranny of the one or in aristocracy towards a tyranny of the few.[1] Nor can there be much doubt, I think, that Mill's point here is thoroughly sound. If it is true that a large proportion of the evils incident to monarchies and aristocracies arise from the sinister interests of their ruling classes (that is, from interests which conflict with the general good of the community), then this will be equally true of democracies, so far as in regard to them, also, it is necessary to recognize the existence of a ruling class

---

[1] Nor is Mill the only man in the early nineteenth century who approaches political theory in this way; this is also the case with J. C. Calhoun, the apologist of the Southern States of America in the years preceding the Civil War; and an interesting comparison may be drawn between Mill and Calhoun on this basis. They both begin by accepting James Mill's argument regarding representative government; they both generalize it in the same way; henceforth they are both constantly preoccupied with the problem of discovering means of qualifying or arresting the tyranny of the majority; but here the similarity ceases. Mill attacks the problem from all conceivable angles and is not disposed to be critical regarding the consistency of the various possible solutions. Calhoun, on the other hand, being cast in the same mould as James Mill, insists on attempting to solve it without going beyond his original premises. Thus, with Calhoun, we seem to be once again in the presence of the tough rigour of the older utilitarians; and it is to this, I imagine, that he owes most of his present popularity in the United States.

whose interests may not be identical with those of the whole community. And it *is* necessary, Mill argues, in so far as it is the majority who rule in a democracy, and the majority of any community is composed of those who live by unskilled or semi-skilled labour.

If follows that the government of a democracy will be under a standing temptation to undertake legislation in the interests of the majority which may not be in the interests of the whole community. They may, for example, attempt to limit competition within the labour market in order to keep up wages; or they may favour the manual worker at the expense of the professional man; or, more generally, they may take up an attitude of determined hostility to any developments which do not conform to their own narrow and rigid standards of human excellence. It is quite irrelevant, as Mill points out, to object that 'none of these things is for the *real* interest of the most numerous class'; it is not what their interests are but what they suppose them to be that is important; and as kings and aristocracies have often taken a very short-sighted view of their interests, it is difficult to see why a loftier mode of thinking should be expected from labour governments.[1]

17. With this enlargement of his father's conception of the problem of government, Mill was inevitably led to look for its solution along lines that had either been unconsidered by his father or considered and rejected. In this sense, therefore, Mill's political theory has to be sharply distinguished from that of the older utilitarians. It is also necessary to distinguish between several different solutions that were offered by Mill at different times. There is one which may be regarded as a reasonable development, in the changed conditions of the nineteenth century, of the solution offered by the older utilitarians; but this is flanked by two others in which Mill explores the possibilities of political theories that are completely opposed to the utilitarian way of thinking.

---

[1] *Representative Government*, chap. 6.

Mill's revised utilitarianism differs from the older version in two main respects. It was a basic principle with the older utilitarians that a person himself was the best judge, and the only trustworthy guardian, of his own interests. But they had not realized or wholeheartedly accepted all the implications of this principle, and Mill spent a good deal of time (very profitably) in drawing attention to the implications that they had neglected. Thus he became one of the most influential pioneers of the female suffrage movement; and then again (although he did not do nearly so much about it) he was also a consistent supporter of the co-operative movement.

Mill further considered that the older utilitarians had a very inadequate idea of what constitutes a person's interests. He waged a determined fight against their cut-and-dried list of the springs of human action. Insisting on the possibility of influencing the ends at which men aim (and not merely the means they employ to attain those ends) he saw, as the older utilitarians could not, a possibility of educating them for democracy by cultivating in them the virtues of justice and self-government. Since he held that the most effective way of educating people for democracy is by exercising them in it, he also taught that democratic institutions themselves are the 'remedy for the worst mischiefs to which a democratic state of society is exposed'; and he never entirely abandoned his belief in the efficacy of this homoeopathic remedy.

18. On the other hand, Mill was never entirely satisfied, either, that homoeopathy was a cure for all the infirmities of democracy. Thus he was led to search among the political theories antagonistic to utilitarianism for means to supplement its deficiencies; and in the conservative theory of Coleridge he found, during his early manhood, two principles that appeared to him to be worthy of support. The first asserted that political societies are the result of a long and gradual process of historical development, in the course of which people must acquire an unquestioning loyalty to some form of political association. The second emphasized the organic nature of the state; pointed to the necessity of a balance among its various classes and of a corresponding balance in its constitution; and asserted, more particularly, that in view of the political incapacity of the multitude it was necessary to combine the control of the government by the many with its actual exercise by the few.

Mill did not long retain his belief in these principles. It ran completely counter to the cast of his mind to suppose that our forms of government are necessarily decided for us by the stage we have reached in the march of history. While he continued, moreover, to retain his belief in the principle of balance, he now began to think of the governing class in terms of bureaucracy rather than aristocracy. Thus the extent to which Mill was influenced by Coleridge gradually diminished. But this does not mean that he was content to acquiesce in all the changes which would result from a democratic régime. On the contrary, he began to devote himself with more and more singleness of purpose to the discovery of means whereby resistance might be kept up to the ruling tendencies of democracy; and in the course of his search he makes many suggestions of varying degrees of merit.

The ruling principle of the essay on *Liberty*, which has come to be more closely associated with Mill's name than any other book, may be called the principle of insulation, or the principle of political monadism. It is similar in some respects to the ancient theory of natural rights. But whereas the old theorists held that certain human interests must be protected from interference because they were connected in some way with the eternal laws of the universe, Mill held that they were to be protected because of 'the absolute and essential importance of human development in its richest diversity'. Thus in his opinion a circle should be drawn round every human being within which his individuality 'ought to reign uncontrolled either by any other individual or by the public collectively'. He infers from this that every person has an absolute right to do as he pleases with whatever he has produced by his own labour and, again, an absolute right to say as he pleases provided that what he does and says makes no difference to other people. But it is impossible to distinguish in this way between that part of a man's behaviour which affects only himself and that which also affects others; nor is it desirable in the interests of genuine individuality to attempt to do so.

19. Thus it would appear that in his political thinking Mill makes use of most of the theories that have been formulated regarding the nature of society and of government. In an age of eclectics he has considerable claim to be regarded as the arch-eclectic. We might compare him to those Victorian architects who were in the habit of designing one part of a building in the Italian style, a second in the Gothic, a third in the Moorish, and so on.

Nevertheless there is no denying that we still have a good deal to learn from Mill. Along with the spurious individuality that he teaches he has also done a lot to elucidate the conditions of genuine individuality. Granted that the essay on *Liberty* is a very muddled book, it still remains notable as containing the most moving and convincing statement of the central political problem of our time. 'The worth of the state in the long run', Mill warns us in the concluding sentence, 'is the worth of the individuals composing it; and a state which dwarfs its men, in order that they may be more docile instruments in its hands *even for beneficial purposes*—will find that with small men no great thing can be accomplished.' Throughout his life this was the problem with which Mill was perpetually concerned. Turning it this way and that he attacked it from all conceivable angles. In so doing he has considerably enlarged our knowledge of the alternatives before us; and in my opinion the moral to be drawn from his teaching is quite unambiguous.

As between the three strands in Mill's political thinking it is the utilitarian strand which yielded the most valuable results. The important consideration here is that in the long run the only dissident elements that have any chance of establishing themselves in a democracy are those which the democracy is willing to tolerate. Hence we come back to the prime necessity of securing an educated democracy. Hence, again, we have to realize that no suggestions for the establishment of centres of resistance to democratic trends are likely to be of any practical value unless they frankly leave the *ultimate* power in the hands of the people. 'Whatever advice, exhortation, or guidance is held out to the labouring classes', as Mill puts it, 'must henceforth be tendered to them as equals, and accepted by them with their eyes open.' But it is precisely this consideration that Mill forgets when he attempts to find safeguards against the tyranny of the majority in a balanced constitution or a theory of indefeasible rights.

MILL'S DOCTRINE OF THE TWO SCHOOLS

1. The actual complexity of Mill's political position, with all its doubts, hesitations, and qualifications, stands in sharp contrast to the simplicity of the terms he usually employs to describe it. According to his own account, the fundamental division among politicians and political theorists is that between conservatives and progressives. As Carlyle had regarded Hume and Dr. Johnson as the two half-men of their time, so did Mill regard Bentham and Coleridge as 'the great seminal minds' who succeeded them. To Bentham it was given, Mill considered, to discern the truths with which existing doctrines and institutions were at variance; to Coleridge the neglected truths which lay *in* them. Since moreover it was in these terms also that the generality of early Victorians thought about politics, Mill and Carlyle in their turn came to be regarded as the two half-men of that age.

Nor was Mill prepared to regard the difference of opinion between conservatives and progressives merely as a political one. 'It was the essence of the Victorian's point of view', observes Lord David Cecil, 'to divide men into sheep and goats. His rigid moral code drove a wedge through the mixed ranks of humanity.' In this way, as in most other ways, Mill was a thoroughly representative Victorian. The sheep for him were those men who made for progress; the goats those who made for reaction; and although he sometimes protests against the error of treating the moral view of actions and characters as if it were the sole one, it always remained dominant for him. He never wrote anything on any subject without considering its bearings on the politics of the day. In his case, therefore, it is quite unnecessary to force the theme of social significance. He was as full of it as any man ever has been.

2. Hence the charges, so frequently brought against Mill by his contemporaries, of unfair dealing in philosophical controversy. As war is sometimes said to be an extension of policy, so philosophy for Mill was an extension of politics. If, then, he sometimes failed to declare his whole mind on some speculative question, he was merely practising in philosophy the usual and necessary reticence of the politician.

A comment of Martineau's, made in the heyday of Mill's influence and reputation, is very much to the point here.

No writer it is possible [says Martineau of Mill] was ever more read between the lines; his authoritative force of intellect, his perfect mastery of his material, his singular neatness of exposition, marked him as a great power in the speculative world. But, as usual, the real interest felt was not less scientific than moral—as to the direction in which that power would work. A certain air of suppression occasionally assumed by Mr. Mill himself, with hints for a revision of the existing narrow-minded morals, has increased this tendency. This suppressive air is the greatest fault we find in him; it is his only illegitimate instrument of power; for it weighs chiefly on the weak: and the shadow which it passes across his face is sometimes so strong as almost to darken the philosopher into the mystagogue.[1]

Nor is it only Mill's opponents who talk in this way. Substantially the same thing is sometimes said of him by his friends—by way of praise rather than blame. Morley, for instance, records that Mill 'was unrivalled in the difficult art of conciliating as much support as was possible and alienating as little sympathy as possible for novel and extremely unpopular opinions'. Hence, as Morley notes with complete satisfaction, Mill 'husbanded the strength of truth and avoided wasteful friction'.[2]

[1] Martineau, *Essays, Reviews and Addresses*, iii. 534 f.
[2] Morley, *Critical Miscellanies*, iii. 421.

3. Seeing then that in Mill's opinion philosophical issues are so intimately related to political issues, it obviously becomes a matter of some importance to determine, (i) how exactly Mill considers them to be related, and (ii) whether in fact they are so related. These are the questions that I propose to discuss in this chapter and the principal texts that I shall make use of are the extremely fine essays that Mill wrote on Bentham and Coleridge in the tolerant period of his early manhood; for having recognized Bentham and Coleridge as the two great political influences of their generation, Mill scarcely hesitates to credit them also with the greatest philosophical acumen. 'Whoever could master the premisses and combine the methods of both', he declares, 'would possess the entire English philosophy of their age.'

With all their differences, Mill points out, Bentham and Coleridge were in complete agreement about one thing. Both made it their occupation 'to recall opinions to first principles', taking no proposition for granted without examining its grounds and ascertaining that it possessed 'the kind and degree of evidence suitable to its nature'. Hence they both agreed in perceiving that the groundwork of all other philosophy must be laid in 'a theory respecting the sources of human knowledge and the objects which the human faculties are capable of taking cognisance of'. Now the prevailing theory of the eighteenth century was that proclaimed by Locke, 'that all knowledge consists of generalizations from experience'; or what in the opinion both of Locke and of Mill comes to the same thing, that 'sensations and the mind's consciousness of its own acts, are not only the exclusive sources but the sole material of our knowledge'. Hence according to this theory there is no knowledge *a priori*—'no truths', as Mill puts it, 'cognisable by the mind's inward light and grounded on intuitive evidence'. Coleridge, however, along with the German philosophers since Kant and most of the British since Reid, takes the opposite view. He admits that no knowledge is possible without experience but he holds that in some cases the visible appearances of nature excite in us by an inherent law ideas of the invisible things on which they depend; therefore he believes that it is possible by direct intuition to perceive things and recognize truths not cognizable by our senses.

4. Among the truths which are thus known *a priori* according to Coleridge are 'the fundamental doctrines of religion and morals, the principles of mathematics and the ultimate laws even of physical nature'. It was indeed precisely because it promised to save these things from the destructive analysis of Locke and his followers that Coleridge valued the intuitionist theory of knowledge. The intuitionists believe with Hume that it is impossible to prove the existence of God from experience. But they do not therefore conclude that we know nothing of God. They prefer to conclude that some of our knowledge is not derived from experience. The derivation of all knowledge from experience, they hold again, can only end in the denial of morality, because it will then be reduced either to the blind impulses of animal sensibility or to a mere calculation of prudential consequences. Finally, they hold that even science, on the theory of Locke, loses its character and becomes empiricism; since a fact is only scientifically accounted for, according to them, 'when we are made to see in it the manifestation of laws which as soon as they are perceived at all are perceived to be necessary'.

On the other hand the followers of Locke retort that the intuitionists 'lay down principles under which a man may enthrone his wildest dreams in the chair of philosophy'. Even if with gross inconsistency the private revelations of a Boehme or a Swedenborg are disavowed (or in other words outvoted) this is still only substituting as the test of truth the dreams of the majority for the dreams of each individual. Indeed it is the peculiar danger of intuitionism that it provides a ready means by which whoever is on the stronger side may dogmatize at his ease and instead of proving his propositions may rail at all who deny them as bereft of 'the vision and the faculty divine' or blinded to its plainest revelations by a corrupt heart. Thus in the battle of the two schools neither side is sparing in its imputation of horrid consequences to the creed of its antagonists. 'The one doctrine is accused of making men beasts, the other lunatics.' And although at this period of his life Mill deprecated such imputations, it was not long before he was again indulging in them.[1]

5. Thus Mill's doctrine of the two schools comprises three main tenets: first, that all differences of opinion on philosophical topics are reducible to a fundamental dichotomy; secondly, that this dichotomy is intimately related to the political differences between progressives and conservatives; thirdly, that it originates in the epistemological difference between experientalists and intuitionists. Mill's references to these two schools are so constant and consistent throughout his life that they appear to be the fixed poles of his intellectual world. Nor, in view of the enormous importance that Mill attaches to the difference between them, should we be surprised to find that his occasional declarations of neutrality on the subject are to be treated with a certain reserve.

He says, for example, that logic 'is common ground on which the partisans of Hartley and of Reid, of Locke and of Kant may meet and join hands'. Regarding his own *Logic*, which is by far the most important of his philosophical books, he declares 'that no proposition in this work has been adopted for the sake of establishing, or with any reference to its fitness for being employed in establishing, preconceived opinions in any department of knowledge or of enquiry, on which the speculative world is still undecided'. But in private his language was apt to be very different.

You have very rightly judged [he wrote to the German translator of his *Logic*] that to give the cultivators of physical science the theory of their own operations was but a small part of the

---

[1] *Dissertations*, i. 397, 331, 394, 396, 403 ff.

object of the book; and that any success in that attempt was chiefly valued by me as a necessary means towards placing metaphysical and moral science on a basis of analysed experience in opposition to the theory of innate principles so unfortunately patronized by the philosophers of your country.

In his *Autobiography* he is equally explicit. 'The German or *a priori* view of human knowledge', he says, 'is likely for some time longer to predominate. But the *System of Logic* supplies what was much wanted, a textbook of the opposite school— that which derives all knowledge from experience.'[1]

Now it is plain that our interpretation and evaluation of the *Logic* will depend a good deal upon which set of these assertions we believe. If we believe the former, we shall expect to find in the *Logic* a series of discussions of traditional logical problems, along more or less traditional lines, with perhaps no very close connexion between them. If we believe the latter (which we are naturally inclined to do, seeing that they were not made for publication in Mill's lifetime) we shall regard the *Logic* as a manifesto of the progressive-experiential school whose programme has been outlined. But there is also a third alternative. It may be that the *Logic* reflects a way of thinking whose fundamental tenets have not been disclosed to us or even, perhaps, consciously realized by its author; and, strange as it may seem, this is I believe the true state of the case; for there are many respects in which Mill's teaching is widely at variance with the description he gives of it—not only in politics but also in logic and epistemology.

6. The doctrine of the two schools was not peculiar to Mill or to the utilitarians. It was widely held in the early nineteenth century that a belief in progress naturally went with the inductive philosophy of Bacon or the new way of ideas of Locke; a belief in order with the intuitive philosophy of

---

[1] *Logic*: Introduction, Sect. 7; Mill to Gomperz (19/8/1854) quoted *New Letters of J. S. Mill, The Times* (29/12/1938); *Autobiography*, p. 190.

Descartes or Kant. The germ of the idea was found in the two political parties which had crystallized out of the troubles of the seventeenth century—the Tories being regarded as the conservative party, the Whigs as the progressive. Thence it was generalized into a division between conservatives and progressives in general—'not only' as Macaulay puts it, 'in politics but in literature, in art, in science, in surgery and mechanics, in navigation and agriculture, nay even in mathematics'.

A systematic age next considered how conservatives and progressives had endeavoured to recommend themselves to the public. Here it was thought that the progressives had encouraged people to weigh the secular advantages of the reforms they advocated, while the conservatives had appealed to their feelings, and particularly to their religious and moral feelings. Thus the conservatives were regarded as the party of religion, the progressives as the party of irreligion; and this provided an easy bridge to a distinction in terms of the arts: the conservatives were the romantics, the progressives the classicists.

This was how the distinction appealed to Mr. Crotchet in Peacock's *Crotchet Castle*. 'The sentimental against the rational, the intuitive against the inductive, the ornamental against the useful, the intense against the tranquil, the romantic against the classical; these', says Mr. Crotchet, 'are great and interesting questions which I should like before I die to see satisfactorily settled.' And this, more or less, was how the situation still appeared to Mill a few years later. 'The Germano-Coleridgian doctrine', he says, 'expresses a revolt against the eighteenth century. It is ontological because that was experimental: conservative because that was innovative; religious because so much of that was infidel; concrete and historical because that was abstract and metaphysical; poetical because that was matter-of-fact and prosaic.'[1]

[1] *Dissertations,* i. 403.

Nevertheless Mill does seem to be introducing a new note into the distinction. The conservative school, we have all along been assured, is intuitive or *a priori*; the progressive is inductive or experimental. But the conservative school we are now told is 'concrete and historical', while the progressive is 'abstract and metaphysical'. Thus the progressive school is inductive and at the same time abstract and metaphysical; the conservative is *a priori* and at the same time concrete and historical. And if this seems hard to understand, it becomes no easier when Mill goes on to say that the members of the Coleridge school were 'the first who inquired with any comprehensiveness or depth into the inductive laws of the existence and growth of human society,'—'the first who pursued in the spirit of Baconian investigation a philosophy of society in the only form in which it is yet possible, that of a philosophy of history'.[1]

7. There are several senses in which the school of Bentham may be described as abstract and metaphysical; several corresponding senses in which the school of Coleridge may be described as concrete and historical:

(i) One of the standing marks of a conservative theory of morals is the tendency to connect a person's duties with his station in society. Burke, for example, assumes that God having 'disposed us and marshalled us, by a divine tactick, not according to our will but according to his, he has in and by that disposition virtually subjected us to act the part which belongs to the place assigned us'. Progressive moralists, on the other hand, make a point of ignoring station when defining duty; and no one has ever gone farther in this direction than Bentham. According to him 'the standard of right and wrong by which alone the propriety of human conduct can be tried' is 'the greatest happiness of all those whose interest is in question'; and among those he includes the lower animals on the same terms as men, since they also can suffer.

[1] *Dissertations*, i. 425 (condensed).

(ii) It is one thing to say that in a matter of duty we should pay no attention to a person's station in society; quite another to say that in point of fact the whole idea of station is unreal because society consists simply of the multitude of persons who compose it. Nevertheless people are prone to connect their ideas of what is and what ought to be, and Bentham's abstract theory of morals is accompanied by an equally abstract theory of society. 'The community', he says, 'is a fictitious body composed of the individuals who are considered as constituting as it were its members. The interest of the community then is, what?—the sum of the interests of the several members who compose it.'

(iii) As the utilitarian ethics is based on the principle that men and other animals are susceptible of happiness, so the utilitarian theory of government is based on the principle that men pursue their own interests and the utilitarian economics on the principle that they prefer a greater gain to a smaller. Its procedure in these studies defines a third sense in which Bentham's school may be described as abstract and the most intelligible sense in which it may also be described as metaphysical. As a subjective idealist, Mill regularly uses the term *metaphysical* as a synonym for *psychological*. The method pursued by the utilitarians is, then, abstract and metaphysical so far as they attempt to explain and evaluate 'social phenomena' on the basis of a few leading principles of human nature.

8. Now one of the characteristic features of Mill's middle period, when he aimed at many-sidedness, was the series of essays in which he recommended the work of some of the men who were then, in the golden age of history, revolutionizing its study.[1] Mill had originally learned something of what history might be from Carlyle; but he soon came to consider

---

[1] *De Tocqueville on Democracy in America* (1840); *Michelet's History of France* (1844); *Guizot's Essays and Lectures on History* (1845). These are all reprinted in *Dissertations*, ii. Mill's best statement about the stages of historical study is in *Michelet*, pp. 124–30.

that the sort of history Carlyle wrote—'the essence of innumerable biographies'—was by no means the highest sort. At a further stage, he considered, history might come to be regarded as 'a progressive chain of causes and effects', or rather as 'a gradually unfolding web'; and although nobody had yet succeeded in constructing 'a science of history' along these lines, he thought that some progress towards it had already been made.

It was on the basis of his discovery of history that Mill characterized the philosophy of Bentham as abstract and metaphysical. 'Bentham's idea of the world', he wrote, 'was that of a collection of persons pursuing each his separate interest and pleasure.' But it was precisely because the *philosophes* of the eighteenth century had the same idea that they failed in their attempt to new-model society. Ignoring the host of civilizing and restraining influences by means of which society is sustained, they did not recognize in many of the institutions which they assailed 'necessary conditions of civilized society though in a form and vesture no longer suited to the age'. Hence they involved many great truths in a common discredit with the errors which had grown up around them, and it looks for the moment as if Mill, like Coleridge, is going to devote his life to the discovery of these neglected truths.[1]

But although Mill repudiates Bentham's doctrine that a community is a fictitious entity reducible to the individuals who compose it, he is as emphatic as Bentham in dissociating the idea of duty from the idea of station and he never had any doubt that the study of society could only attain the status of a science when it was based upon psychology. Thus of the three senses in which Bentham's philosophy may be described as abstract and metaphysical, Mill accepted the criticism of the Coleridge school only in regard to one; and even on this point he soon saw reasons for modifying his attitude.

[1] *Dissertations*, i. 362, 424, 461 ff.

9. The trouble with historians, from the reformer's point of view, is that they find it difficult to believe that social arrangements can be different from what they actually are. Few of them indeed go to the lengths of Carlyle and assert that whatever is, is right. In order to arrive at that conclusion a man needs also to have a very lively sense of the presence of God in the things of this world. But even an historian with as purely secular an outlook as Macaulay is apt to be impatient with the discussion of rights which are unaccompanied by mights. Nor is it difficult to understand why this should be so. The first principle of the historian must be that nothing happens accidentally; hence, regarding forms of government as a sort of organic growth or spontaneous product of any given state of society, he will tend to conclude that in the main we must take governments as we find them.

Whatever is the strongest power in any society, he will argue, will obtain the governing authority; and a change in the political constitution cannot be durable unless it is preceded or accompanied by an altered distribution of power. Therefore, apart from details, political organization or reorganization is not susceptible to the direction of philosophical reformers. According to Macaulay, for instance—

Constitutions are in politics what paper money is in commerce. They afford great facilities and convenience. But we must not attribute to them that value which really belongs to what they represent. They are not power, but symbols of power, and will in an emergency prove altogether useless unless the power for which they stand be forthcoming.[1]

Now this 'organic' or 'naturalistic' view of government, as Mill calls it, was plainly not one to which he could subscribe for long. He might refuse to go the whole way with Bentham and his father who looked upon a 'constitution in the same light as a steam plough or a threshing machine'. But he

---

[1] Macaulay, *Miscellaneous Writings* (1860), i. 375.

could not but believe that within certain limits 'institutions and forms of government are a matter of choice' and that therefore 'to inquire into the best form of government is not a chimerical but a highly practical employment of scientific intellect'. He admitted, indeed, that political machinery has to be worked by men and even by ordinary men; and that it would be a great mistake, accordingly, for any legislator not to take advantage of existing habits and feelings. Nevertheless he held that people can acquire new habits and feelings, particularly when they are incited thereto by enlightened leaders; and it is this consideration which provides him with the basis of his reply to Macaulay.

It is what men think [he says] that determines how they act and though the persuasions and convictions of average men are in a much greater degree determined by their personal position than by reason, no little power is exercised over them by the persuasions and convictions of those whose personal position is different and by the united authority of the instructed. When therefore the instructed in general can be brought to recognize one social arrangement as good and another as bad, very much has been done towards giving to the one or withholding from the other that preponderance of social force which enables it to subsist.[1]

10. A radical reformer, that is to say, may find it useful to point to the accidental genesis in interest and experience of the opinions of the average men who are his opponents or potential converts. But he must believe that he himself, as one of the instructed, whose convictions are founded upon reason, has gone to the root of the matter; otherwise he will be unable to sustain the fervour or exercise the authority required of him; and this consideration suggests that, in regard to the connexion between politics and epistemology, the position at the beginning of the nineteenth century was rather more complex than Mill usually allowed for.

To begin with there was a certain incoherence in both the

[1] *Representative Government* (1861), pp. 15 f.

schools he describes. The radical school held that all knowledge is derived from experience and yet based its political theory on statements regarding human nature which it regarded as having a validity far beyond that which attaches to the empirical generalizations of the conservatives. The Tory school of Coleridge and Carlyle, on the other hand, for all its *a priori* theory of knowledge relied largely on observation of the actual behaviour of man for its formulation of those statements regarding the course of history which formed the immediate basis of its political programme.

Moreover, there was a third school, of Whigs, of a sufficiently conservative turn of mind to be consistently opposed to radicalism, who yet managed to dispense largely or altogether with the *a priori*. They included such men as Burke, Mackintosh, and Macaulay, who, although seldom mentioned by name in Mill's writing, occupied a large place in his thoughts. One of them, Macaulay, was the author (in Mill's words) of 'the bitterest and ablest attack' ever publicly made on his father; another, Mackintosh, was the recipient of an equally wholehearted attack by his father; and the standing charge levelled by the utilitarians against these men was precisely the same as the charge levelled by the intuitionists against them—that namely of empiricism.[1]

11. It has been so much the fashion to talk of the empiricism of Mill—Höffding even speaks of his 'absolute empiricism'—that some surprise may be occasioned by the statement that empiricism was not only a charge levelled against Mill but also one that he levelled against other people. Yet his own usage on the point is completely consistent. He always proclaimed himself an adherent of the School of Experience as against the School of Intuition. Nevertheless he always used the term *empiricism* to denote a theory which he did not hold but which Macaulay, for instance, did. Thus he speaks of

[1] *Autobiography*, pp. 133 f. See also Mill's Preface to his father's *Analysis of Mind* (1869), pp. xvii.

'empiricism and unscientific surmise'; of 'bad generalization or empiricism properly so-called'; of 'knowledge both scientific and empirical'; of 'direct induction usually no better than empiricism'; of 'the empirical method of treating political phenomena which would have recognized Kepler but would have excluded Newton and Laplace'. Had he foreseen the way in which his own name would be linked with empiricism, he would doubtless have said of himself what he said of Bacon—

The philosopher who laboured to construct a canon of scientific induction, by which the observations of mankind, instead of remaining empirical, might be so combined as to be made the foundation of safe general theories, little expected that his name would become the stock authority for disclaiming generalization and enthroning empiricism, under the name of experience, as the only solid foundation of practice.[1]

Now Mill's use of the terms *empirical* and *empiricist* is, I take it, conformable to common usage.[2] If, moreover, an appeal is made to precedent it is plain that a man need not be, or at least need not *choose* to be, an empiricist, even although he is an experientialist. Locke's is an obvious case in point. Nobody has ever insisted more strenuously than he that all our ideas are derived from experience. Nobody has ever at the same time drawn the line more sharply between certain knowledge and probable opinion. Bacon's is an even more interesting case. For one thing his general position is extremely close to Mill's. Both begin by recognizing a single alternative to the method of experience; but in both cases this divides into

[1] *Logic*, vi. 10. 8, v. 5. 3; *Political Economy*, v. 7. 2; *Comte and Positivism*, p. 121; *Autobiography*, p. 157; *Examination of Hamilton*, p. 627 footnote.

[2] Thus Venn in the Preface to his *Empirical Logic* says, 'By the introduction of the term *Empirical* into the title, I wish to emphasize my belief that no ultimate objective certainty, such as Mill for instance seemed to attribute to the results of Induction, is attainable by any exercise of the human reason.'

two as soon as the method of experience is elaborated; and
the result is that the one and only true method of experience
finds itself with an enemy on the left as well as an enemy on
the right. Bacon writes, for example—

Those who have practised the sciences have been either empiricists
or dogmatists. The empiricists, like the ants, merely collect and
use: the rationalists, like spiders, spin webs out of themselves.
But the way of the bee lies in between: she gathers materials from
the flowers of the garden and the field and then by her own powers
transforms and digests them; and the real work of philosophy is
similar.[1]

The other interesting point about Bacon is that, unlike
Mill, he distinguishes between a legitimate and an illegitimate
method of experience without having had much opportunity
of seeing what they would produce in practice, and indeed
without fully availing himself of the limited opportunity he
had. It was, in fact, by the sort of anticipation of nature that
he most deprecated that Bacon arrived at the conclusion that
the empirical kind of philosophy would produce 'even more
deformed and monstrous theories than the rationalist kind'.
All the later philosophers of experience had Newton's *Principia* before them as a norm of science and scientific method. It
was on this model accordingly that some of them attempted
to create the new science of political economy. Their appreciation of Newton's work, moreover, was heightened by the
fact that some of their most eminent and successful opponents
attacked them not in the name of intuition at all but rather in
the name of experience. Hence it became necessary for the
utilitarians to argue that the principles taught by these men
were not derived from experience in the correct way; and as
they, however mistakenly, made much of Bacon, the utilitarians tended to shelter under the rival authority of Newton.

12. The general position, then, is that Mill, like Bacon and
Locke, wants to be an *experientialist* but he does not want to

[1] Bacon, *Novum Organum*, Lib. i, Aph. 95, 64.

be an *empiricist*. This seems to mean that while he holds that experience provides all the material of knowledge, he also holds that there are various ways of dealing with this material, some of which lead to bad and unscientific conclusions and others to safe and scientific conclusions. He suggests that it is unscientific and unsafe to deal with the observations of experience directly and piecemeal, scientific and safe to deal with them more indirectly and in combination with one another. Finally he regards as an empiricist a man who, failing or refusing to recognize any distinction between the scientific and the unscientific ways of treating experience, inevitably treats it in the unscientific way.

Thus the general question that arises concerning Mill's *Logic* is : How successful was he in combining an acceptance of experientialism with a repudiation of empiricism? The answer is that he was not at all successful. So far as he really appealed to the teachings of experience (as in his doctrine of the syllogism) he was constrained to admit that any conclusions arrived at by reasoning must always be uncertain. So far as he really made out a case for believing that certain conclusions can be arrived at in science (as in his doctrine of induction) he relied upon assumptions about the hidden causes of phenomena which lie completely outside the realm of experience.

Hence Mill's *Logic* divides fairly sharply into two parts. Considering the sort of antagonists by whom he was faced, it is not difficult, moreover, to understand the distribution of topics within these parts. Empiricism was associated in Mill's mind with the political theories of such men as Burke, Mackintosh, and Macaulay; intuitionism with those of Coleridge, Carlyle, and Whewell. The first group were Whigs, the second Tories. But there was also another difference between them. The strength of the first group lay in political theory and history. The strength of the second group was derived from all sorts of other studies whose findings had

been represented as relevant to political theory. In particular Whewell had written extensively on mathematics and
science; and the tendency, if not the intention, of his efforts,
Mill was convinced, was 'to shape the whole of philosophy,
physical as well as moral, into a form adapted to serve as a
support and a justification to any opinions which happened to
be established'.[1]

Now it is this difference in the spread of Mill's two groups
of opponents that determined which parts of the *Logic* should
be predominantly anti-intuitionist and which parts anti-
empiricist. As the strength of the Whig group was confined to
politics, the anti-empiricist polemic in the *Logic* is mainly
to be found in Book VI, *Of the Logic of the Moral Sciences*,
and to those parts of Book III, *Of Induction*, which lay the
foundation for Book VI. On the other hand, having come to
the conclusion that the chief strength of intuitionism lay 'in
the appeal which it is accustomed to make to the evidence of
mathematics and of the cognate branches of physical science',
Mill was primarily concerned in the *Logic* to meet it on
this ground. Hence he pursued his attack on intuitionism in
Book II, *Of Reasoning*, and in those parts of the other Books
which support or extend the argument of Book II. Indeed, he
pressed this attack so far, and with so little fear of the consequences, that his position here is generally regarded as a
standard exposition of empiricism.[2]

[1] *Dissertations*, ii. 453.
[2] *Autobiography*, p. 191.

V

BACKGROUND OF INDUCTION

1. I N his *Autobiography* Mill gives a pretty complete account of how he wrote his *Logic*, and if the various references to induction are gathered together,[1] three results stand out. In the first place, the problem with which he was specifically concerned was that of reducing the conditions of inductive proof 'to strict rules and to a scientific test, such as the syllogism is for ratiocination'. He regarded as his principle opponents men like Comte and Whewell (and in the *Logic* itself he adds Whately and Macaulay) who either ignored this problem altogether or else denied the possibility of solving it. And he was convinced not only that the problem could be solved but that he had solved it. In the second place, the order in which Mill treats the various topics included in induction is not the order in which he originally considered them. He began with the theory of the social sciences which is expounded in Book VI, and it was only after a considerable interval that he felt himself competent to attempt the generalization of the methods used in the physical sciences which is contained in Book III. But in the third place, Mill always thought of the possibilities of social science in terms of the actual achievements of physical science. He solved his major difficulty regarding the philosophy of politics, not by any direct consideration of concrete political problems, but by reflecting on the distinction between chemical composition and mechanical mixture. And the names he gives to the various methods used or proposed in the investigation of social affairs are immediately indicative of his indirect approach to the subject. Thus he speaks of Macaulay's chemical or experimental method, of Bentham's geometrical or abstract

[1] *Autobiography*, pp. 133 ff., 154, 175 ff.

method, of his own physical or concrete deductive method, and of Comte's inverse deductive or historical method.

We may then, I suggest, be in a better position to understand Mill's theory of induction, as he himself understood it, if we reverse the ordinary procedure and read the *Logic* backwards, beginning with Book VI and ending with Book III. And the principal thing we have to understand here, I would also suggest, is the basis upon which Mill thought it possible to construct a demonstrative theory of inductive proof.

2. It is true that there are passages in the *Logic* which represent a different and, it may well be thought, a more tenable attitude towards induction. At one point, for example, Mill lays it down that 'the most scientific proceeding can be no more than an improved form of that which was primitively pursued by the human understanding while undirected by science'. When mankind first formed the idea of studying phenomena according to a stricter and surer method than they had hitherto practised they did not, he points out, set out from the supposition that nothing had been already ascertained. What they did was to correct one generalization by means of another; and any other procedure, he considers, was rigorously impracticable. 'Experience', he says, 'must be consulted in order to learn from it under what circumstances arguments from it will be valid—All that art can do is but to give accuracy and precision to this process, and adapt it to all varieties of cases, without any essential alteration in its nature.'[1]

Nor does Mill hesitate, on occasion, to draw attention to the inevitable corollary of this position. If the correction of one generalization by another is 'the real type of scientific induction', he holds, we must always be prepared to revise our generalizations when the progress of knowledge shows their truth to be contingent on some circumstances not

[1] *Logic*, iii. 4. 2.

originally attended to; whence it follows that in matters of evidence, as in all other human things, 'we are unable to obtain the absolute'.[1]

His usual attitude is, however, quite different. 'Induction', he also says, 'is proof; it is inferring something unobserved from something observed; it requires therefore an appropriate test of proof and to provide that test is the special purpose of inductive logic.' 'The business of inductive logic', he says again, 'is to provide rules and models (such as the syllogism and its rules are for ratiocination) to which if inductive arguments conform those arguments are conclusive and not otherwise.' And he declares it to be 'the express object' of that part of the *Logic* which deals with induction to provide these rules and models.[2]

3. Nor can there be much doubt that Mill arrived at this conception of inductive logic as he says he did by way of a determined attempt to lay a firm foundation upon which political theories could be constructed. Like Locke's *Essay concerning the Human Understanding*, with which it has so many other points in common, Mill's *Logic* originated in the discussions of a small study-circle. A group of young men of the utilitarian persuasion, who had formed a class to learn German, continued it in order to study Political Economy, Logic, and Psychology—the key sciences of the utilitarians. They used to meet, to the number of a dozen or so, at Grote's house in Threadneedle Street two mornings a week, from half past eight to ten, on their way to work; and their rule was to discuss thoroughly every point raised, whether great or small, until every person present had arrived at a conclusion with which he was satisfied. Most of what Mill subsequently did 'to rationalise and correct the principles and distinctions of the school logicians' in Book I of the *Logic* originated in these discussions. The immediate result was

---

[1] *Logic*, iii. 21. 4.
[2] Ibid. iii. 2. 5; iii. 9. 6; Preface to the 1st ed., footnote.

an able and surprisingly appreciative criticism of Whately's *Elements of Logic* which appeared in the *Westminster Review* in 1828.

The next part of the *Logic* to be thought out was that which deals with the social sciences. Macaulay's famous articles on James Mill's *Essay on Government* were now running in the *Edinburgh Review* and causing considerable stir among the utilitarians who had long regarded Mill's *Essay* as (in the words of his son) 'a masterpiece of political wisdom'. But while young John Mill was convinced from the beginning that Macaulay was wrong in standing up for 'the empirical mode of treating political phenomena against the philosophical', he also felt that there was truth in some of Macaulay's strictures on his father's *a priori* method. So setting himself the task of thinking out the proper method for the advancement of social science he drafted the essay, *On the Definition and Method of Political Economy* which afterwards appeared in his *Unsettled Questions concerning Political Economy* and was the basis, with some modifications, of Book VI of the *Logic*.

At this point, however (after having worked out or failed to work out this theory of the syllogism), Mill was brought to a halt, 'on the threshold of induction', for lack of a comprehensive view of the physical sciences. Nor was it until five years later, when Whewell published his *History of the Inductive Sciences*, that he obtained what he wanted. Under the impulse provided by this book he quickly re-read Herschel's *Discourse on the Study of Natural Science* and in the short space of two months completed the greater part of Book III of the *Logic—On Induction*. Thus Mill had been working on the *Logic* for some ten years before he began to write on induction—from, say, 1828 when he reviewed Whately until 1837 when Whewell published his *History of the Inductive Sciences*. During that time he had acquired, and partly expressed, a set of very definite opinions regarding the nature of the universe and of science; and it was on the basis of these opinions, which are very sketchily indicated in the *Logic* itself, that he built his theory of the experimental methods.

4. Macaulay's great merit is that in criticizing the political theory of the utilitarians he goes to the root of the matter and concentrates upon the logic of their arguments. 'The utilitarians', he notes, 'have sometimes been abused as intolerant, arrogant, irreligious—as enemies of literature, of the fine arts, and of the domestic charities.' But he was convinced that almost all their peculiar faults arose from the systematic way in which they ignored the teachings of experience in favour of *a priori* argument. James Mill's *Essay on Government*, for example, was an elaborate treatise from which, but for two or three passing allusions, it would not appear that the author was aware that any governments actually existed among men. 'Certain propensities of human nature are assumed, and from these premisses the whole science of politics is synthetically deduced.' And this procedure appeared to Macaulay to be completely wrong for two reasons.[1]

In the first place there were, in Macaulay's opinion, no propositions which are absolutely and universally true of human nature except one—that men always act from self-interest; and this, he maintains with considerable show of reason, is not only a true but an identical and therefore a completely useless proposition. When therefore we see the actions of a man we know with certainty what he thinks his interest to be; but it is impossible to reason with certainty from what we take to be his interest because there is nothing which may not become an object of desire to somebody.

Macaulay's second objection takes the form of a dilemma which is closely and significantly related to Mill's difficulty regarding the syllogism. He draws attention to the fact that although the utilitarians pretend to deduce their conclusions

---

[1] Macaulay, *Miscellaneous Writings* (1860), i. 360 f., 285. The quotations in the following paragraphs will be found on pp. 317, 345 f., 321.

regarding politics from the underlying springs of human nature rather than from the mere surface of experience, they nevertheless claim that their knowledge of these underlying springs is drawn from experience. Thus the question arises, what is the extent of this experience? and more particularly, does it include experience of the political behaviour of men? And any answer to this question, Macaulay argues, must explode the pretensions of the utilitarian reasoning. If it is said that our knowledge of the principles of human nature draws upon our experience of the political behaviour of men, it follows that 'our knowledge of human nature instead of being prior to our knowledge of the science of government will be posterior to it'; and the utilitarians will then be con-victed of arguing in a circle. If, on the other hand, we have not in our formulation of the principles of human nature taken account of the political behaviour of men, then these principles will be defective, and any theory of politics deduced from them will be erroneous.

Thus Macaulay came to the conclusion that the science of politics was to be arrived at, not by the method of deduction after the manner of the schoolmen and the utilitarians, but by the method of induction after the manner of Bacon, or, at least, after what he took to be the manner of Bacon.

Proceeding thus [he claims], patiently, diligently, candidly, we may hope to form a system of politics as far inferior in pretention to that which we have been examining and as far superior to it in real utility, as the prescriptions of a good physician, varying with every stage of every malady and with the constitution of every patient, are to the pill of the advertising quack, which is to cure all human beings, in all climates, of all diseases.

And this was a remark that Mill never forgot and only partially forgave.

5. Bain refers to the 'highly seasoned rhetoric' of Macau-lay's articles and even Sir Ernest Barker thinks that although they are lively and trenchant, they are in some places 'rhetorical and superficial'. J. S. Mill, however, was under no delusion about the strength of Macaulay's case or the weakness of his father's answer. 'He treated Macaulay's attack', Mill says of his father, 'as simply irrational; an attack upon the reasoning faculty; an example of the saying of Hobbes, that when reason is against a man, a man will be against reason'; and he adds that this made him think that there was something 'more fundamentally erroneous' in his father's conception of philosophic method as applicable to politics than he had hitherto supposed.[1]

Nevertheless it was Macaulay's errors rather than his father's that Mill was more concerned to stress in his own contribution to the controversy. His father was indeed mistaken, Mill thought, in basing his theory of government on a single proposition about the nature of men—that they always seek their own selfish interests. He was also mistaken in supposing that there is some one form of government which would fit all societies; and this was indeed a pretension meriting the ridicule with which it had been treated by Macaulay. But Macaulay, he holds, was much more mistaken in objecting to political reasoning which is grounded on principles of human nature and demanding instead that it be based on the observation of political facts; since it should be evident to anybody familiar with experimental science, in Mill's opinion, that no political conclusions of any value can be arrived at in this manner.

Suppose, for instance, that we are inquiring into the effects of the Corn Laws.

Though it may be perfectly certain, from theory [Mill holds] what *kind* of effects Corn Laws must produce, and in what general direction their influence must tell upon industrial prosperity; their effect is yet of necessity so much disguised by the similar or

---

[1] Bain, *James Mill*, p. 230; Barker, Introduction to James Mill's *Essay on Government* (Cambridge), p. xxi; J. S. Mill, *Autobiography*, p. 134.

contrary effect of other influencing agents, that specific experience can at most only show that, on the average of some great number of instances, the cases where there were Corn Laws exhibited the effects in a greater degree than those where there were not.

The number of instances necessary to afford a fair average can never, he adds, be obtained; and the circumstances which prevent our drawing a conclusion from experience in this case, he argues, are present in all political inquiries. We can only generalize from experience regarding the cause of a given effect when the state of affairs we are trying to understand is always the effect of some one cause; and we can only generalize regarding the effect of a given cause when that effect is distinguishable from the effects of all other causes. But these are precisely the circumstances according to Mill that are most conspicuously absent in social affairs. 'There plurality of causes exists in almost boundless excess and effects are for the most part inextricably interwoven with one another.' Hence Mill concludes that induction from specific experience is out of the question in this sphere.[1]

6. But how, then, are we to acquire any knowledge of the laws which govern society? 'Since it is vain to hope', Mill replies, 'that truth can be arrived at while we look at facts in the concrete, clothed in all the complexity with which nature has surrounded them, there remains no other method than the *a priori* one.' Therefore, as no other method remains, that must be the method; otherwise there would be no hope of constructing a science of society at all; and this was a possibility that Mill never dreamed of entertaining. Thus he held that an *a priori* approach to the problems of society must be feasible, in spite of what Macaulay had said, on the ground that an *a posteriori* approach, such as Macaulay had recommended, was not feasible; and in some of his statements on the subject he goes even further than his father.[2]

---

[1] *Logic*, vi. 9. 6; iii. 10. 8.
[2] *Unsettled Questions on Political Economy*, p. 148.

'As the surface of history affords no certain principles of decision', says James Mill, 'we must go beyond the surface and penetrate to the springs within.' 'The laws of the phenomena of society', says J. S. Mill, 'are and can be nothing but the laws of the actions and passions of human beings united together in the social state.' 'Human beings in society', he goes on, 'have no properties but those which are derived from and may be resolved into the laws of individual man.' 'Social science, therefore,' he concludes, 'is a deductive science. It infers the laws of each effect by considering all the causes which conjunctly influence the effect and compounding their laws with one another.'[1]

It is true that Mill does not always take quite such a high line. He goes on to recognize that 'the ground of confidence in any concrete deductive science is not the *a priori* reasoning but the accordance between its results and those of observation *a posteriori*'. Hence he is led to admit verification as an essential constituent of the method. Admitting also that it is immaterial whether we begin with the reasoning or with the observation he is led, again, to recognize the legitimacy in social science not only of the physical or concrete deductive method but also of what he calls the inverse deductive or historical method. In the former, the conclusions deduced from our knowledge of human nature are afterwards verified by specific experience; in the latter, 'we begin by obtaining them provisionally from specific experience and afterwards connect them with the principles of human nature'.[2]

But these modifications do not, to Mill's mind, constitute the concessions to Macaulay's point of view that they might appear to be, and he continued to inveigh against it to the end of his life. In the *Logic* he remarks with lofty acidity that 'the vulgar notion that the safe methods on political subjects are those of Baconian induction . . . will one day be quoted

[1] James Mill, *Essay on Government*, p. 16; J. S. Mill, *Logic*, vi. 7. 1, vi. 9. 1. (condensed).   [2] *Logic*, vi. 9. 1.

amongst the most unequivocal marks of a low state of the speculative faculties in any age in which it is accredited'. In the *St. Andrews Address*, a quarter of a century later, he simply repeats the teaching of the *Logic*. 'In politics', he says again, 'it is evident to whoever comes to the study from that of the experimental sciences, that no political conclusions of any value for practice can be arrived at by direct experience. Such specific experience as we can have serves only to verify, and even that insufficiently, the conclusions of reasoning.'[1]

7. Thus, according to Mill, no progress can be made in the development of a concrete science of sociology except by way of the construction of various abstract sciences, of the type of political economy which determines how men *would* act if they were moved solely by some particular kind of motive.[2] In order therefore to determine how men *will* act in any concrete situation which calls various motives into play, it is necessary to combine the findings of the various abstract sciences which deal with these motives. But in advocating this view of social science, it is evident that Mill has entirely reverted to Bentham's conception of human nature and is far, far away from the doctrine, endorsed in his principle of

---

[1] Ibid. iii. 10. 8; *St. Andrews Address*, pp. 50 f.

[2] 'Geometry', says Mill, 'presupposes an arbitrary definition of a line as that which has length but not breadth. Just in the same manner does political economy presuppose an arbitrary definition of man, as a being who invariably does that by which he may obtain the greatest amount of necessaries, convenience, and luxuries, with the smallest quantity of labour and physical self-denial. . . . The conclusions of political economy, consequently, like those of geometry, are only true, as the common phrase is, *in the abstract*' (*Unsettled Questions*, pp. 144 f.). It may be noted that it is on the basis of this definition that Ruskin launched his attack on Mill's political economy. It is, Ruskin argues, as if we were to construct a science of gymnastics in which we assumed that men had no skeletons and demonstrated on this supposition 'that it would be advantageous to roll the students up into pellets, flatten them into cakes, or stretch them into cables'. Hence Ruskin concludes that the idea that political economy, as understood by its Victorian practitioners, is of any practical value is 'perhaps the most insolently futile of all that ever beguiled men through their vices' (*Unto this Last*—Everyman, pp. 115, 141 f.).

individuality, that the man makes the motive and not the motive the man.

Why, then, when all Mill's deepest sympathies were on the other side did he persist in advocating this view of social science? Granted that his position is a survival from the teaching of Bentham and James Mill, why should he continue to submit to their influence here when he had repudiated it in so many other parts of his philosophy? The answer is, I believe, that on this point Mill felt that the older utilitarians had the backing of the teaching of physical science. He continued, then, to share their view of social science because he concurred in their convictions regarding the constitution of the universe at large; and it was from these cosmological assumptions, again, that he derived his general theory of induction.

It is a current belief [says Halévy] that the English are cautious observers with a keen eye for detail, careful to respect the complexity of nature. This belief, however, is far from the truth. In reality, simplification has been the distinctive note of British thought during the nineteenth century. British men of science united the inexperience and the boldness of the self-taught man. They are reasoners, who sought and discovered simple laws, men of intuition, who claimed to perceive beneath the manifold of natural phenomena, the outline of a machine whose parts are few, and whose motions are all sensible. It was because it was at once the simplest hypothesis and the most easily visualized that Dalton adopted the atomic theory. And the method of Bentham and his school was Dalton's method applied to the moral sciences.[1]

8. Now suppose a man in the early nineteenth century to set himself the task of elucidating and defending this notion of science. Suppose, again, that he presents his findings, as he has ample precedent for doing, in the form of a system of logic. What, under these circumstances, will be the main features of his system?

---

[1] Halévy, *History of the English People in 1815*, Pelican Edition, iii. 208.

In the first place, his sympathy with the traditional formal treatment of the subject is going to be extremely limited. He will be concerned above all with the 'modes of investigating truth and estimating evidence by which so many important and recondite laws of nature, in the various sciences, have been aggregated to the stock of human knowledge'.[1] He will be interested therefore, not only in the processes by which true conclusions may be arrived at from true premisses but also in the processes by which true premisses are acquired to begin with. Hence, while he will certainly endeavour to incorporate into his system of logic as much of the traditional theory as may be useful to him, he will insist on restating it from his own very different point of view.

In the second place, he will be inflexibly opposed to any suggestion that there may be modes of arriving at truth equal or superior to those of the scientist. Thus although he may take considerable interest in the developments of history that were occurring in his time parallel to the developments of science, he is bound to distinguish sharply between the value of these developments. History for him will be merely descriptive while science is explanatory. Consequently he will look forward to the time when the findings of the historian can be verified, or even perhaps anticipated, by the deductions of the sociologist.

In the third place, he has somehow to reconcile the constant appeal to experience that he finds in contemporary scientists with their quest for certainty by reference to an underlying reality; and this, it is plain, is not going to be an easy thing to do. For while the scientists continually referred to this reality; they were not prepared, as practical men, to be very interested in it for its own sake. They would have regarded any such preoccupation as savouring of mysticism, and for their part they were content to concentrate on the control of appearances. The consequence is that a thick cloud of

[1] *Logic*, Preface, p. vii.

ambiguity lies over their whole conception of the relation between the reality and its appearances. Indeed, they frequently speak as if the reality were itself an appearance, to be distinguished from other appearances merely by a process of analysis. (As Halévy puts it, they claim 'to perceive beneath the manifold of natural phenomena, the outline of a machine whose parts are few *and whose motions are all sensible*'.) Nevertheless, obscure though it may be, something intelligible has to be made of this distinction between the surface of experience and the underlying reality, since it is the central conception of nineteenth-century science. Nor do we have to dig very deep to discover that it is also the central conception of Mill's doctrine of induction.

9. We have seen that, in Mill's opinion, the two great difficulties which obstruct the investigation of social affairs are the plurality of causes and the intermixture of effects. According to the former, the same kind of phenomenon is not always produced by the same cause: the effect a, that is to say, may sometimes arise from A and sometimes from B. According to the latter, the effects of different causes are often not dissimilar but homogeneous and marked out by no assignable boundaries from one another: A and B, that is, may produce not a and b but different portions of one effect a.[1]

Now the deductive method provides no safeguard against a possible plurality of causes; not indeed is there any certain remedy against this difficulty. It might, it is true, be evaded if science were confined to ascertaining the effects of given causes and excluded from ascertaining the causes of given effects; but it is scarcely practicable to suggest that it should be so confined;[2] and as soon as any attempt is made to ascertain the cause of a given effect, there is only one precaution that can be taken. The investigator must multiply his ob-

---

[1] *Logic*, iii. 10. 1.

[2] Nevertheless Mill does make the suggestion at one point. Ibid. v. 3. 7.

servations of *a* in the hope that, if it has any other cause beside *A*, he will eventually come across an instance of it. Thus, as Mill recognizes, it is 'only when the instances, being indefinitely multiplied and varied, continue to suggest the same result that this result acquires any high degree of independent value'. But it would obviously be incorrect to maintain that any multiplication of instances, however extensive and varied, could ever be relied upon with complete assurance to have excluded the possibility of an unobserved plurality of causes. Hence when he actually comes to the point, Mill is careful to speak only of the 'virtual' or 'practical' certainty obtained by a conclusion after a 'sufficient' number of instances have been observed.[1]

Having reduced it to these dimensions, however, Mill ceases to worry about the difficulty presented by the plurality of causes. Nor should any stress be laid on his occasional suggestion that this difficulty as well as that presented by the composition of causes is to be overcome by the deductive method. He usually thinks of deduction as a method to be practiced only after the possibility of a plurality of causes has been practically excluded by means of the theory of chance. Thus the difficulties raised by the plurality and by the composition of causes are, in Mill's opinion, to be dealt with on two different levels. Plurality is a possibility which can and should be dealt with on the 'empirical' level, but composition, being far more subtle and pervasive, can only be dealt with on the 'explanatory' or 'scientific' level. There 'the separate effects of all the causes continue to be produced, but are compounded with one another and disappear in one total'. The typical instance is that of a body kept in equilibrium by two equal and contrary forces.[2]

---

[1] Ibid. iii. 10. 2.

[2] Ibid. iii. 10. 5; iii. 6. 2. Strictly speaking the composition of causes, in Mill's terminology, is only one of two modes in which the intermixture of effects may occur. In the other mode, the separate effects of the causes cease entirely and are succeeded by phenomena altogether different and

10. Now the composition of causes raises both a practical and a theoretical problem. The practical problem is to find a method of distinguishing the effects of the separate causes when they are, to all appearances, indistinguishably merged into one total effect. The theoretical problem is to provide an intelligible account of the status of the laws of the separate causes; and the scope of this problem becomes clear when we consider the language that has to be used in connexion with the theory of the composition of forces, which is the form assumed by the composition of causes in physics.

The laws of the separate forces, according to this theory, are fulfilled quite as much when they are counteracted by other forces as when they are left to their own undisturbed action. Thus it cannot be stated as a law of nature that a body to which a force is applied *moves* in the direction of that force, because sometimes the body will not move at all and sometimes it will move in a different direction. Nor, for similar reasons, can it be said that the body *moves* with a velocity proportional directly to the applied force and inversely to its own mass. 'To accommodate the expression of the law to the real phenomena we must say not that the object moves but that it *tends to move* in the direction and with the velocity specified.' Similarly all the other laws of the physical world require to be stated in terms 'affirmative of tendencies only and not of actual results'.[1]

Thus the theory of the composition of causes involves a fundamental dualism. On the one hand we have a phenomenal world of 'actual results'; on the other a real world of 'tendencies'. The former depends wholly on the latter but reflects it very imperfectly, and that is why in physics, as in

governed by different laws. Thus in cases of this kind, 'the resulting phenomenon stands forth undisguised, inviting attention to its peculiarity'; and when the *elements* of which it is said to be composed are regarded rather as the *causes* of its production, it presents no particular difficulty to experimental inquiry. *Logic*, iii. 10. 4.

[1] Ibid. iii. 10. 5, cf. *Unsettled Questions*, pp. 161 f.

politics, it is unsafe to reason from the surface of experience. The passage from appearance to appearance can only be made with safety by way of the underlying tendencies, that is, by the deductive method.

11. The deductive method, moreover, may be used for the purpose either of discovering a law or of explaining a law already discovered. A particular fact is explained when we can state the law or laws of which it is an instance. Similarly a law is explained by stating the law or laws 'of which that law is but a case and from which it could be deduced.'[1] But while this might appear to imply that laws which explain and those which are explained (or are to be explained) differ merely in degree of generality, Mill actually holds that there is another difference between them; and he considers this difference to be so important that he marks it by a set of technical terms which he uses with considerable consistency. Laws which explain but are not themselves susceptible of explanation are called *ultimate laws* or *laws of nature* or *laws of causation*; laws, on the other hand, which have been explained or which require explanation are *derivative laws* or *descriptions*; while laws which have not been explained but which require explanation are *empirical laws*.

The typical description for Mill is Kepler's law—that the planets move in elliptical orbits. The typical explanation is Newton's theory that they are moved by the composition of a centripetal force towards the sun along with a projectile force away from it; and *hence* that they move in elliptical orbits. The distinction between a description and an explanation is that different descriptions of the same phenomenon may both be true 'as far as they go', but different explanations cannot both be true. The circular theory of the motion of the planets, for example, describes their general features perfectly well; and thus, although the eliptical theory has a great advantage over the circular in point of simplicity, we cannot say that the

---

[1] *Logic*, iii. 12. 1; iii. 12. 6.

former is true and the latter false. If, however, we consider an alternative explanation to the Newtonian doctrine of gravitation, like the Cartesian theory of vortices, this is precisely what we do have to say.[1]

Now scientific inquirers, Mill finds, give the name *empirical law* to any uniformity which observation and experiment have shown to exist, but on which they hesitate to rely in cases varying much from those which have been actually observed, 'for want of seeing any reason *why* such a law should exist'. It is implied, therefore, in the notion of an empirical law not only that it is a derivative but also that it is an unreliable law; and Mill now proceeds to justify this implication.[2]

12. In the last resort the substantial part of the universe, as Mill sees it, consists of a number of 'permanent causes' or 'original natural agents' like the projectile force of a planet or the attraction exerted on it by the sun. He is by no means sure, indeed, that these agents are quite as eternal as their names suggest. But, at any rate, he considers that we can give no account of their origin, and he also considers that we can discover no regularity in their distribution. 'We not only do not know', he says, 'of any reason why the sun's attraction and the force in the direction of the tangent co-exist in the exact proportions that they do, but we can trace no coincidence between it and the proportions in which any other elementary powers in the universe are intermingled.' Thus the 'utmost disorder' prevails in the distribution of the permanent causes. Nevertheless everything that happens in the universe is subject to law, for, as Mill explains, 'when each agent carries on its operations according to a uniform law even the most capricious combination of agencies will generate a regularity of some sort, as we see in the kaleidoscope,

---

[1] *Logic*, iii. 2. 4. Mill has confused his argument here by using, for his own purposes, the term *induction* as a synonym for *explanation*.

[2] Ibid. iii. 16. 1. Mill's authority for this use of the term 'empirical law' seems to be Herschel. See his *Discourse on Natural Philosophy*, sect. 187.

where any casual arrangement of coloured bits of glass produces by the laws of reflexion a beautiful regularity in the
effect'.[1]

It follows from this conception of the universe that, saving
the superhuman powers of calculation required, everything
that has subsequently happened might have been predicted
by anyone acquainted with 'the original distribution of all
natural agents, and with the whole of their properties, that is,
the laws of succession existing between them and their
effect'. It also follows that these are the only really reliable
laws in the universe. The motion of a planet, for example,
depends on the co-existence of the attraction of the sun and
the original projectile force of the planet; Kepler's law is
therefore reducible to the laws of these forces *plus* the fact
of their co-existence; consequently it might have been false
while Newton's theory remained true, if only the ratio between
these forces had been different. Even when a derivative uniformity holds between different effects of the same permanent
cause, it will still be less reliable than the law of the cause
itself. If *a* and *b*, for instance, accompany or succeed each
other as effects of cause *A*, *b* and not *a* may be defeated by a
counteracting cause; or, again, there may be another cause
B capable of producing *a* but not *b*; and in either case *a* will
only be followed or accompanied by *b* when it is produced
by *A*.[2]

It is in these circumstances that Mill finds the justification
for the limited degree of reliance which is placed on empirical
laws. As an empirical law is a derivative law whose derivation
has not yet been discovered, we cannot be certain that it will
be reliable beyond the limits of time, place, or circumstance
in which it has been found true by observation. Hence we
must discover 'the explanation, the *why* of the empirical law',
in order that we may know under what conditions it will cease

[1] *Logic*, iii. 16. 3; iii. 15. 8.
[2] Ibid. iii. 5. 8; iii. 16. 2; ii. 16. 9; iii. 19. 1.

to be fulfilled. On the other hand, it is important that we should ascertain as many as possible of the empirical laws of phenomena in order 'to facilitate the verification of theories obtained by deduction'. Thus Kepler's laws provided the means of verifying Newton's theory and, as in this case, the ascertainment of empirical laws often precedes their explanation by a long time.[1]

In the next chapter I shall endeavour to show that this cosmological doctrine of Mill's provides the foundation upon which he erects his theory of the experimental methods. In the following chapter I hope to show that it also provides the foundation for his theory of experience.

[1] *Logic,* iii. 16. 4; iii. 11. 3; iii. 16. 1.

VI

INDUCTION BY ELIMINATION

1. At the beginning of his account of induction Mill summarily defines it as generalization from experience. 'It consists', he says, 'in inferring from some individual instances in which a phenomenon is observed to occur, that it occurs in all instances of a certain class, namely in all which resemble the former in what are regarded as the material circumstances.'[1] In point of fact, however, the whole purport of Mill's argument regarding induction is that in some cases at least we may replace this definition by another, and that is how he endeavours to combat the widespread scepticism of his predecessors and contemporaries regarding the possibility of formulating a demonstrative theory of induction.

Twist it how you will, you can never prove from your experience of some particular instances favourable to a universal proposition that all are favourable, since there will always remain the possibility (unless you enumerate *all* the instances) that other instances will turn up which are unfavourable to it. So long, therefore, as induction is defined in terms of generalization, any inductive conclusion will always be at the mercy of a single unfavourable instance. But suppose that you cease to regard the universal as a collection of particulars and, instead, regard the particular as a collection of universals. Your problem is immediately and completely transformed. It is no longer a question of constructing universals out of particulars but of determining what universals in one particular are connected with what universals in another particular. Provided, again, that you are in possession of some information regarding the relations of these universals to one another, you are in a position to turn the contradictory

[1] *Logic*, iii. 3. 1.

H

instance from an enemy into an ally. But we are, according to Mill, entitled to regard particulars as collection of universals since every phenomenon is the expression of a set of underlying tendencies; we are also in possession of some information about the relation of these universals to one another, since they are joined together in the constancy of causation; and it is upon the basis of these assumptions that he formulates his canons of induction.

It follows, he argues, that in the case of causal laws, induction may be regarded not as generalization from experience as he originally defined it, but rather as 'a process of analysis' which may in certain circumstances be regarded as having the same demonstrative force as the syllogism. As the cases in which the redefinition of the inductive process is possible concern the fundamental laws of nature from which all others are deducible, he considers himself entitled, moreover, to represent this new definition as covering the whole field of induction. It must, however, be admitted that Mill was in too much of a hurry to make use of his argument to be explicit, or even consistent, about many of the points in it; and it may, I think, be made more intelligible if it is stated in rather more general terms than he usually employs.[1]

2. According to traditional logical theory, there are only two relations which hold between particular and universal propositions with the same subject and predicate, namely, subalternation and contradiction. Correspondingly, it has been generally thought that there are only two possible ways of arriving at universal propositions on the basis of our experience of particular instances, namely, induction by simple enumeration and induction by elimination. The former endeavours to establish a universal proposition directly by enumerating a number of particular propositions which are

[1] *Logic*, iii. 6. 3; iii. 7. 1. In the following attempt to state the argument underlying Mill's experimental methods, I have been greatly helped by Nicod's analysis of induction.

favourable or subalternate to it. The latter endeavours to establish a universal proposition indirectly by disproving other universal propositions, and it does that by enumerating particular propositions which are unfavourable or contradictory to them.

Thus, failing induction by enumeration, which can never certainly prove a law of nature, it is necessary to rely on induction by elimination, that is by contradiction. But contradiction, it is plain, can only be used to prove a proposition if it is one of a group of propositions, of which one is true. Then if we can disprove all but one of this group of propositions by the discovery of instances which contradict them, it will follow that this one is true. Thus the problem of proving a law of nature, as Mill wishes it to be proved, reduces to two problems. It is necessary, to begin with, to obtain a group of propositions concerning the facts under consideration of which one is true; then it is necessary to disprove all but one of them by the discovery of contradictory instances; and Mill solves these problems by the aid of four assumptions—two theoretical and two practical.

3. The theoretical assumptions summarize his account of the constitution of the universe in terms of primitive causes and the laws of their agency. According to the first theoretical assumption, 'The whole of the present facts are the infallible result of all past facts and more immediately of all the facts which existed at the moment previous.' According to the second theoretical assumption, this great uniformity may be resolved into simpler uniformities in such a way that every element in the antecedent is related by a causal law to some element in the consequent, and every element in the consequent is similarly related to some element in the antecedent.[1]

---

[1] This is the assumption which Keynes has called 'the hypothesis of atomic uniformity', according to which any total change is 'compounded of a number of separate changes each of which is due to a separate portion of the preceding state'. *Treatise on Probability*, pp. 248 ff.

Hence the question now is: 'How to resolve this complex uniformity into the simpler uniformities which compose it?'

Now the order of nature as it is initially perceived presents at every instant 'a chaos followed by another chaos'. Thus we must begin by 'decomposing' each chaos into 'single facts', so that the chaotic antecedent is seen as a multitude of distinct antecedents and the chaotic consequent as a multitude of distinct consequents. After that we must effect 'a separation of the facts from one another not in our minds only but in nature', so that by varying the circumstances we may be able to meet with some of the antecedents (or consequents) apart from the rest and observe the consequents (or antecedents) by which they are succeeded (or preceded).[1] Thus, according to the first practical assumption, we are able to describe the state of the entire universe at any given moment and at any immediately preceding (or succeeding) moment. According to the second practical assumption, we are able to separate these elements and vary their combinations. And with these preliminaries settled we are in a position to state Mill's general argument. In order, however, to take account of the distinction between universals and particulars, which Mill consistently neglects in his doctrine of induction, it seems desirable to use a different set of symbols from his.

4. To say that any event X is the cause of another event Y is to say, according to Mill, that X immediately precedes Y and whenever an event like X in certain respects (say x) occurs, an event like Y in certain respects (say y) will also occur. Hence if every event has a cause, then, in regard to any event Y with a characteristic y, there is always among the immediately preceding events some event, or some combination of events, X with a characteristic x, such that all cases of x are cases of y.

It follows that if we enumerate all the events, and all the possible combinations of events, immediately preceding Y

[1] *Logic*, iii. 7. 1 and 2.

(X', X'', X''', &c.) we shall obtain a group of propositions (all x' are y; all x'' are y, &c.) one of which is true. Hence in order to prove a proposition regarding the cause of a given event it is sufficient (i) to enumerate all the events, and all the possible combinations of events, immediately preceding that event, so as to obtain an exhaustive list of its possible causes; (ii) to prove, in regard to all but one of them, that it cannot be the cause of the given event, since events like it are not always followed by events like the given event. And Mill's experimental methods are designed to contain directions for making use of such contradictory instances in various circumstances.

Thus when it is a question of determining the cause of a given event, it is by means of the Law of Causation—that every event has a cause—that Mill arrives at the group of propositions without which it would be impossible to use for proof the power of contradiction for disproof. When, on the other hand, it is a question of determining the effect of a given event, he uses the principle (which he never explicitly formulates but which may, by analogy with the Law of Causation, be called the Law of Effectuation) that every event has an effect; and his argument then proceeds similarly. It is assumed, that is to say, in regard to any event X (with a characteristic x) that there is always among the immediately *succeeding* events, some event, or combination of events, Y (with a characteristic y) such that all cases of x are cases of y. It follows that if we enumerate all the events which immediately succeed X (Y', Y'', Y''', &c.) we shall obtain a group of propositions (all x are y'; all x are y'', &c.) of which one is true; and Mill's experimental methods also contain instructions for disproving all but one of these propositions in various circumstances.

5. A good deal of the criticism that has been levelled at Mill's theory of induction has turned on the wavering account he gives of induction by simple enumeration and of its relation to induction by elimination. The effect of this criticism has been, as I believe, to obscure rather than to clarify the nature of Mill's theory. But I propose to examine it before proceeding to what I regard as a more pertinent and profitable line of comment.

The proof required of any scientific law depends for Mill upon the sort of law it is. If it is a *description*, then, as it pretends to no truth which it may not share with other descriptions, it requires no proof other than confirmation in particular instances. Thus, regarding Kepler's various hypotheses about the orbit of Mars, he says, 'In all these cases verification is proof; if the supposition accords with the phenomena there needs no other evidence of it.' With an *explanation* like Newton's theory of gravitation, however, the case is different. As it pretends to an exclusive truth, it is not sufficient to show that it leads to a true result. It has also to be shown that 'a false law cannot lead to a true result'; or, in other words, that 'no other law can lead deductively to the same conclusion which that law leads to'. Nor is the position altered if, besides accounting for the facts previously known, a suggested explanation leads also to the prediction of previously unknown facts which experience subsequently confirms. As it accounts for the known facts (and, unless it did, it would have no initial plausibility) it is 'nothing strange', Mill argues, if it accounts for one fact more. On the other hand, the prediction of previously unknown facts can no more assure us of the exclusive truth of a proposed law of nature than its confirmation by known facts.[1]

Thus the possibilities of proof in regard to *empirical laws*, according to Mill, are quite different from those in regard to *laws of nature*. Not being explanatory, they do not require submission to the test of elimination; and not being causal, they do not admit of it. In regard to them, therefore, we are necessarily thrown back upon simple enumeration. And the

[1] *Logic*, iii. 14. 4 and 6.

fact that this is a fallible operation, Mill generally considers
to be of little importance in so far as the precarious inferences
derived from it 'are superseded and disappear from the field
as soon as the principle of causation makes its appearance
there'.[1]

6. There is, however, a difficulty here, or, at least, most of
Mill's critics have thought so, and he sometimes shared their
opinion. It is not only in regard to empirical laws that we are
thrown back on simple enumeration, but also in regard to all
laws which are not causal laws; and therefore in regard to
those assertions about causal laws upon which Mill bases his
account of the experimental methods. The difficulty is, then,
that in order to provide a firm foundation for the experimental
methods it seems necessary to assert that we have a certain
knowledge of these propositions; and as this cannot be provided by the methods (because they depend on it) it would
seem to follow that it must be provided (if at all) by the
fallible method of simple enumeration.

It is because of this difficulty that Mill sometimes speaks
with an uncertain voice regarding the possibilities of simple
enumeration. So far as he regards it as a rival to induction by
elimination he dismisses it very lightly; so far as he regards it
as a necessary basis of elimination he sometimes rates its
possibilities very highly. 'Popular notions', he writes, 'are
usually founded on induction by simple enumeration; in
science it carries us but a little way. We are forced to begin
with it; we must often rely on it provisionally, in the absence
of means for more searching investigation. But, for the
accurate study of nature, we require a surer and more potent
instrument.' Yet he also holds that while the results of simple
enumeration are 'delusive and insufficient' with regard to
some propositions, they are 'certain' with regard to others,
such as the Law of Causation and the first principles of
mathematics. And it is on this basis that he arrives at the

[1] Ibid. iii. 18. 4.

odd conclusion that simple enumeration is not an 'invalid' process but merely a 'fallible' one.[1]

The principle Mill relies on here is that 'the precariousness of the method of simple enumeration is in inverse ratio to the largeness of the generalization'; and he arrives at it by developing his account of empirical laws. When a fact has been observed a certain number of times, he has laid down, we shall in general err grossly if we affirm it as a universal truth. Nevertheless we are perfectly justified in affirming it as an empirical law true within certain limits of time, place, and circumstance. Now the reason for not extending it beyond these limits is 'that the fact of its holding within them may be a consequence of collocations which cannot be concluded to exist in one place because they exist in another'. Hence if we find (i) that the subject-matter of any generalization is so widely diffused that there is 'no time, no place and no combination of circumstances but must afford an example either of its truth or of its falseness'; (ii) that it is always true; then we may conclude, Mill argues, that its truth cannot be dependent on any collocations except those which exist at all times and places. Thus at this point where an empirical law is coextensive with all known experience, 'the distinction between empirical laws and laws of nature vanishes'; any such propositions, consequently, are entitled to a place among the most firmly established truths of science; and applying this argument to the Law of Causation, Mill comes to the conclusion that as it stands at the head of all observed uniformities 'in point of universality' so also does it 'in point of certainty'.[2]

7. It is, however, impossible for Mill to be content for very long with this solution—at the cost of the distinction between empirical laws and laws of nature; and in fact he renounces it almost immediately. The reasons for relying on the Law of Causation, he hastens to add, do not hold in circumstances

[1] *Logic*, iii. 3. 2.
[2] Ibid. iii. 21. 3.

unknown to us and beyond the possible range of our experience. Hence it must be received 'not as a law of the universe but of that portion of it only which is within the range of our means of sure observation with a reasonable degree of extension to adjacent cases';[1] that is to say, it must be received after all *not* as a law of nature but *merely* as an empirical law; and with this admission Mill may be regarded as recognizing that it is impossible to make anything demonstrative out of simple enumeration.

But what then is to be said of induction by elimination? If its first principles have only the evidence of simple enumeration which is not demonstrative, then, the critics urge, it cannot be demonstrative either. Hence they infer that Mill's theory of induction by elimination is involved in a common ruin with his theory of induction by simple enumeration. This inference is, however, I think, mistaken. Granted that we have, and can have, no certain knowledge of the truth of Mill's first principles, the results obtained by his experimental methods will still be certain provided that his first principles are *in fact* true, and that they are *in fact* capable of being applied as he claims they can be applied. And although Mill might with advantage have been clearer on this point, he does in his best statements define his position in a way which eludes the common criticism.

All ultimate laws [he says, for example] are laws of causation, and the only universal law beyond the pale of mathematics is the law of universal causation, namely, that every phenomenon has a phenomenal cause. It is on the universality of this law that the possibility rests of establishing a canon of induction. A general

---

[1] Ibid. iii. 21. 4. It may be noted that while Mill asserts in the first two editions of the *Logic* that induction by simple enumeration 'may in some remarkable cases amount to full proof', he alters this in later editions to read that it 'may amount practically to proof' (iii. 3. 2). Nevertheless he continues to assert that 'in the case of a law so completely universal as the law of causation' the evidence of simple enumeration 'amounts to the fullest proof' (iii. 24. 4).

proposition inductively obtained is only then proved to be true when the instances on which it rests are such that, if they have been correctly observed, the falsity of the generalization would be inconsistent with the constancy of causation.[1]

I conclude, therefore, that there are only two grounds upon which it is possible to criticize Mill's claim to have established a demonstrative theory of induction. It may be argued either that causation is not constant, as he says it is, or else that we cannot prove that the falsity of some proposed inductive generalization would be inconsistent with that constancy, as he says we can. To sustain the former objection it would be necessary to controvert the whole cosmological theory out-lined in the previous chapter; to sustain the latter it is only necessary to consider the consistency of Mill's theory of the experimental methods with that cosmological theory. I propose to confine myself here to this easier task.

8. One principal question remains over from Mill's account of the deductive method: how, namely, are we to discover, and *prove* that we have discovered, those laws of nature that he assumes to be at work beneath the surface of experience? And at this point Mill's argument takes an unexpected turn. So far his treatment of induction has rested upon the inaccessi-bility to observation of these laws of nature; and on this basis he has persistently belittled the work of observers like Kepler in favour of that of theorists like Newton. But now, assuming apparently that the underlying tendencies are capable of coming to the surface of experience, he asserts that 'the mode of ascertaining these laws neither is nor can be any other than the four-fold method of experimental enquiry'. He admits, indeed, that the premisses of the deductive method 'will doubt-less make their first appearance in the character of hypotheses not proved nor even admitting of proof'. But he holds that this, though their initial, can never be their final state. 'To enable an hypothesis to be received as one of the truths of

[1] *Comte and Positivism*, p. 58.

nature', he says, 'and not as a mere technical help to the human faculty, it must be capable of being tested by the canons of legitimate induction and must actually have been submitted to that test.' Hence he reaches the paradoxical conclusion that a science can only be rendered deductive 'by means of a new and unexpected induction'.[1]

Paradoxical as this conclusion may be, however, it is not difficult to see how Mill arrives at it. In order to prove a law of nature, as distinct from an empirical law, it is necessary, according to his way of thinking, to show not only that this law covers all the facts but that no other law can. Thus the question—*the* question of inductive logic as Mill understands it—is: how may this be done? And he endeavours to answer it by representing induction as a process of analysis rather than generalization. Instead of regarding the universal as a collection of particulars, he now regards the particular as a collection of universals; hence he has no longer to construct universals out of particulars but merely to determine the causal connexion between universals in different sets of particulars; and in doing this, he builds upon the assumption that 'the whole of the present facts are the infallible result of all past facts, and more immediately of all the facts which existed at the moment previous'. 'Here then', he says, 'is a great sequence which we know to be uniform. The question is, how to resolve this complex uniformity into the simpler uniformities which compose it, and assign to each portion of the vast antecedent the portion of the consequent which is attendant on it.'[2]

9. Thus in order to reduce the problem of induction to a process of analysis, Mill has to assume that we are able to describe the state of the whole universe at the moment immediately preceding (or succeeding) the event whose cause (or effect) is under investigation. And the obvious objection is that, failing omniscience, we are unable to do this. It is true, as Mill points out, that in most inquiries we have reasons for

---

[1] *Logic*, iii. 11. 1; iii. 13. 7.   [2] Ibid. iii. 7. 1.

believing that information regarding some parts of the universe would be irrelevant even if we had it. In making chemical experiments, for example, we do not think it necessary to note the position of the planets, because experience has shown that 'that circumstance is not material to the result'. But this consideration does little to obviate the difficulty; for although our disregard of some of the facts may be based on knowledge, our disregard of others is plainly due to ignorance. Moreover, even if it were entirely based on knowledge it could only be based on the present and presumably imperfect state of our knowledge; and this is fatal to the claim that the results of the methods of elimination can ever be certain.[1]

Nor is this by any means the whole of the difficulty by which Mill is faced when he attempts to prove that the falsity of some particular causal law would be inconsistent with the general constancy of causation. If he is to prove that, it is necessary not only that he should enumerate all the events immediately preceding (or succeeding) any event but also that he should state them in terms of their ultimate elements. For unless we are dealing, in the premisses of the methods, with the ultimate elements of nature, they can only yield empirical laws in which the statement of ultimate tendencies is inextricably intertwined with the assumption of contingent facts.[2]

This requirement, moreover, applies not only to our statement of the events among which we are to seek for the cause (or effect) of a given event; it also applies to our statement of the given event itself. Thus in order to apply the experimental

---

[1] *Logic*, iii. 7. 1.

[2] Ibid. iii. 10. 1. This assumption is also implied by the requirement that we must enumerate all the events that *immediately* precede (or succeed) a given event. For unless we are dealing with 'ultimate events' or 'single facts', it is nonsense to talk of *immediate* succession and we shall have to recognize, what experience appears to teach, that it is always possible to discover an intermediate event between any event and any other event.

methods we have, in Mill's language, to 'decompose' the whole universe into 'single facts'. This means that we have to suppose that we have already disentangled all the complications produced by the composition of causes and penetrated beneath the surface of experience to its underlying tendencies. Hence it may be charged against Mill's experimental methods, as it was by several of his contemporaries, that they can only be used to obtain the results that Mill expects from them when there is no longer much need to use them.

10. 'Upon these methods', says Whewell, 'the obvious thing to remark is that they take for granted the very thing which it is most difficult to discover, the reduction of the phenomena to formulae such as are here presented to us.' Venn points out that the state of affairs postulated by the methods is not 'a definite amount of knowledge surrounded by an indefinite extent of ignorance', but rather 'an indefinite extent of knowledge broken by a definite gap of ignorance'; and he draws attention to the enormous assumptions involved in what he calls 'the alphabetical view of the universe', by means of which 'every student in an examination can now undertake to exhibit to us the exact process by which physical antecedents are eliminated, and the true *cause* of any phenomenon is determined'. But Jevons perhaps gets as near to the root of the matter as anybody when, after remarking on the obscurity which has been introduced into science and philosophy by the supposition 'that the knowledge of causes is something different from other knowledge and consists, as it were, in getting possession of the keys of nature', he observes that in Mill's *Logic* 'the term *cause* seems to have re-asserted its old noxious power'.[1]

Mill, in short, knows nothing of the 'mysterious step' that Whewell talks about by means of which the scientist passes from the observation of particulars to the discovery of the

---

[1] Whewell, *Philosophy of Discovery*, p. 263; Venn, *Empirical Logic*, pp. 410, 358, 403; Jevons, *Principles of Science*, pp. 221 f.

universals by which they are related. For him the universe is already neatly arranged in piles of universals. Consequently the only problem involved in scientific discovery, as he sees it, is the problem of sorting out connexions between universals; and it is this way of looking at the subject that accounts, I believe, for the air of unreality that hangs over his whole treatment of it. As Bacon wrote about science like a Lord Chancellor, so Mill wrote about it like an eminent official of the East India Company who had to find the answers to the most intricate Indian problems in the papers before him in London. Such examples of his experimental methods as he gives were added as afterthoughts, and most of them were suggested by Bain who knew as little about scientific discovery at first hand as Mill.[1]

11. Jevons is fully entitled, moreover, to speak of Mill's notion of causation, and consequently of science, as one that had been repudiated by most British philosophers. In some respects indeed Mill's may be regarded as the central position in the nineteenth century, since he neither denies the distinction between description and explanation with the positivists nor magnifies it into a distinction between the natural and supernatural with the volitionists (see Chapter X). In regard, however, to the point which he regards as of fundamental importance in inductive logic, he is contradicted equally by both parties. So far as *natural laws* are concerned, they both assert the impossibility of going beyond a description of the facts, and they both therefore deny the possibility in *natural science* of any mode of inductive proof other than the confirmation of hypotheses by favourable instances.

Nor was this meeting of extremes a new thing in philosophy. Hume and his arch-opponent, Reid, had already reached a similar agreement in the eighteenth century. 'No philosopher', says Hume, 'who is rational and modest has ever pretended to assign the ultimate cause of any natural operation. It is

[1] *Autobiography*, pp. 207 f. footnote; Bain, *J. S. Mill*, pp. 66f.

confessed that the utmost effort of human reason is to reduce the principles productive of natural phenomena to a greater simplicity, and to resolve the many particular effects into a few general causes by means of reasonings from analogy, experience and observation.' 'Those philosophers', says Reid, 'seem to have had the justest views of nature as well as of the weakness of human understanding, who, giving up the pretence of discovering the causes of the operations of nature, have applied themselves to discover, by observation and experiment, the *rules* or *laws* of nature, according to which the phenomena of nature are produced.'[1]

Going still further back this was also the attitude of Locke, whose philosophy was associated with the rise of science in so many ways. He himself tells us that in the age of a Boyle, a Sydenham, the great Huygenius, and the incomparable Mr. Newton, he regarded it as 'ambition enough to be employed as an under-labourer in clearing the ground a little and removing some of the rubbish that lies in the way of knowledge'. But for all that he was remarkably open-minded both about the achievements and about the possibilities of science. 'As to a *perfect* science of natural bodies (not to mention spiritual beings) we are, I think,' he says, 'so far from being capable of any such thing that I conclude it lost labour to seek after it.'[2]

12. It is not surprising, then, that Mill's attempt to formulate a demonstrative theory of induction, which would produce such a *perfect* science both of natural bodies and of spiritual beings, should have been opposed by nearly everybody when he first published his *Logic*. In spite of the slighting manner in which he sometimes speaks of Bacon, his theory is, indeed, very like Bacon's; and there was, it is true, an enormous interest in the work of Bacon at this time. But even

[1] Hume, *Enquiry concerning Human Understanding*, sect. iv, part 1; Reid, *Essays on the Active Powers*, Essay iv, chap. 3.
[2] Locke, *Essay*, Epistle to the Reader; iv. 3. 29.

such an ardent Baconian as Macaulay considered that 'it was not by furnishing the philosophers with rules for performing the inductive process well, but by furnishing them with the motive for performing it at all', that Bacon conferred so vast a benefit upon society. And this was the general opinion. Whately thought that any rules which could be laid down for induction 'must always be comparatively vague and general and incapable of being built into a demonstrative theory like that of the syllogism'. Herschel regarded the help afforded to the scientist by the Baconian methods as 'more apparent than real'.[1]

What is surprising at first sight is Mill's enormous success in changing public opinion on this point. In a few years his *Logic* was adopted as a textbook in most British universities; and it was generally held that his treatment of induction constituted the most valuable part of it. But this also becomes intelligible enough when we consider how exactly Mill had fashioned his theory to suit the spirit of the age. 'It was an age', as Mill himself notes, 'destitute of faith but terrified of scepticism.' And one great advantage of his theory of induction was that it promised to save men from scepticism, in regard to science at least, without apparently requiring from them very much in the way of faith. When one looks into the matter, indeed, it is plain that Mill's theory of induction also requires a good deal of faith. But it was not necessary for the Victorians to make any effort to swallow Mill's assumptions, because his cosmological outlook was also, for the most part, theirs. By this time the Newtonian physics had been taught, popularized, and applied for a century and a half; it had changed not only the industrial but the intellectual life of the country; and, whatever he may say to the contrary, it is on the basis of a popular Newtonian view of the universe, interpreted in a

---

[1] For the contemporary interest in Bacon see Fowler, *Bacon's Novum Organum*, p. 148. Macaulay, *Critical and Historial Essays* (Everyman), ii. 387; Whately, *Elements of Logic*, iv. 3. 3; Herschel, *Discourse*, sect. 192.

Platonic sense, that Mill attempted to provide rules and models for induction, such as the syllogism and its rules are for ratiocination.

13. It is true that Mill is sometimes at great pains to assure us that the constancy of causation he has in mind consists in nothing but the fact that 'the phenomena of nature takes place according to invariable laws of succession'. It is also true that it is essential to his conception of the role of causation in induction that he should insist on this. If it concerned anything but phenomena, he would not be able to use the constancy of causation to provide him with the groups of propositions required for elimination. Hence at the beginning of his account of induction in the *Logic*, Mill is careful to leave no shadow of doubt on this point.

> I premise, then [he says], that when in the course of this inquiry, I speak of the cause of any phenomenon, I do not mean a cause which is not itself a phenomenon; I make no research into the ultimate or ontological cause of anything. The law of causation, the recognition of which is the main pillar of inductive science, is but the familiar truth that invariability of succession is found by observation to obtain between any fact in nature and some other fact which has preceded it.[1]

No sooner, however, has he laid this down than he has to contradict it. It is necessary to our using the word *cause*, he now points out, that we should believe not only that the antecedent always *has* been followed by the consequent but that it always *will* be so; for there are many sequences, like that of day and night, which are 'as uniform in past experience as any others whatever', but which yet cannot on this account be regarded as cases of causation at all but only 'as conjunctions in some sort accidental'. 'Invariable sequence, therefore,' Mill holds, 'is not synonymous with causation, unless the sequence, besides being invariable is unconditional.' Hence, taking account of the need of allowing for the composition

---

[1] *Logic*, iii. 5. 2.

of causes, he is finally led to assert that causal laws are statements not about 'actual results' but about 'underlying tendencies'.[1]

Thus the idea of cause, by means of which Mill hoped to arrive at a canon of induction combines, and necessarily combines it would seem, two contradictory notions. On the one hand, the cause is the underlying tendency, and to state the causes of things is to state those ultimate laws of nature which can never reveal themselves unambiguously on the surface of experience. On the other hand, the cause is nothing but a phenomenon, and to state the cause of anything is merely to state an antecedent on which that sort of thing is always consequent. Unless the cause were the ultimate reality, there would be no reason to believe that one and only one conclusion regarding it can be drawn from a given set of facts. All science would be merely descriptive and we could never do better than guess until a guess is found which tallies with the facts. But unless at the same time the cause is also a fact which appears among the facts constituting the premises of the inductive inference, no conclusion can be drawn from them at all.

[1] *Logic*, iii. 5. 6; iii. 10. 5.

VII

RELATIVITY OF KNOWLEDGE

1. IN the preceding chapters an account has been given of Mill's doctrine of induction comprising his theories both of the deductive and of the experimental methods. It has been shown that this doctrine depends upon an elaborate set of cosmological assumptions. It has also been shown that Mill arrived at these assumptions by generalizing Newton's account of the physical universe, with a view to justifying the abstract and metaphysical approach to political theory characteristic of the utilitarians.

The political theories of the older utilitarians were abstract and metaphysical in that they attempted to deduce the behaviour of men in communities from a few leading principles of human behaviour which they regarded as having a validity independent of and superior to history. Thus their theory of government was deduced from the principle that men always pursue their own interests; their economic theory from the principle that men always prefer a greater gain to a smaller. James Mill never failed to damn any fact which conflicted with a theory of his. J. S. Mill himself remarks of Bentham that he had 'to find a principle which he could assume as self-evident and to which he could attach all his other doctrines as logical consequences' because 'systematic unity was an indispensable condition of his confidence in his own judgment'.[1]

Nor, although Mill finds fault with the inflexibility of the political formulae of the older utilitarians, can his own approach to the subject (in theory at any rate) be regarded as any less abstract and metaphysical than theirs. On the contrary he only succeeds in formulating more flexible methods

[1] *Dissertations*, i. 385.

by emphasizing still further the contrast they had drawn between the fluctuating appearances and the abiding reality of the universe.

2. The question with which Mill is concerned in Book VI of the *Logic* is, he tells us, 'Whether moral and social phenomena are really exceptions to the general certainty and uniformity of the course of nature; and how far the methods by which so many of the laws of the physical world have been numbered among truths irrevocably acquired and universally assented to, can be made instrumental to the formation of a similar body of received doctrine in moral and political science.' In order to answer that question he had in the latter part of Book III considered how these laws had been acquired; and he had come to the conclusion—traditional among the utilitarians—that it was by means of the deductive method as practised by Newton. 'To it', he says, 'we owe all the theories by which vast and complicated phenomena are combined under a few simple laws which could never have been detected by their direct study.' It, therefore, was destined henceforth irrevocably to predominate in the course of scientific investigation; and, in fact, a revolution was already peaceably and progressively effecting itself in philosophy, the reverse of that to which Bacon had attached his name. 'That great man', says Mill, 'changed the method of the sciences from deductive to experimental and it is now rapidly reverting from experimental to deductive.'[1]

Now the deductive method, according to Mill, consists of three operations. In the first, the separate tendencies of the causes jointly responsible for a set of complex phenomena are determined; in the second, the joint effects of various combinations of these tendencies are calculated; in the third, the results obtained are verified by direct observation. These operations do not necessarily occur in this order. When verification precedes the other operations, Mill speaks of the

[1] *Logic*, Preface, p. viii; iii. 11. 3; iii. 13. 7.

method involved as the inverse deductive or historical method; when it does not, he speaks of the physical or concrete deductive method. But in either case, and this is the important point, Mill thinks of the deductive method as involving a transition from one stage or level of knowledge to another. At the empirical level, empirical laws or descriptions, like Kepler's law, are ascertained by direct observation. At the explanatory level, laws of nature, like Newton's theory of gravitation, are established and the empirical laws are deduced from them and from collocations of fact.

Thus, at the empirical level, the best we can hope for is the discovery of derivative uniformities in which the statement of ultimate tendencies is inextricably mixed up with the assumption of ultimate facts. It is because of the unresolved facts involved in empirical law that they are also called descriptions; and because they are descriptions, it is held that they can only be trusted within narrow limits and that they can never pretend to a truth which they may not have to share with similar laws. At the explanatory or scientific level, however, the aim of the scientist, according to Mill, is to extricate the tendencies from the facts and by this means to arrive at laws of nature which have an exclusive and ultimate truth. Hence the basis of the distinction between the laws enunciated at the two stages is that the former only happen to be true because of the collocations of fact which obtain in this world, while the latter, being independent of all such collocations will be true of all possible worlds.

3. It would appear, then, that the characteristics of some parts of Mill's philosophy are very different from what he represents them to be. As he describes his own position, he is a progressive in regard to politics and an experientialist in regard to knowledge. Consequently his fundamental antagonism is to dogmatism in politics and to intuitionism in theory of knowledge, under which comprehensive term he includes all those theories of knowledge, from the rationalism of

Descartes to the transcendental idealism of Kant, which do not stem directly from Locke's way of ideas. In point of fact, however, his fundamental antagonism over large stretches of his writing is to opportunism in politics and to empiricism in theory of knowledge; and he endeavours to combat them by means of a cosmological doctrine which is very similar in many respects to that of Plato.

Consider, for example, Mill's own account of Plato's theory of forms; read *forces* for *forms*, and you have a substantially accurate account of the assumptions upon which Mill bases his whole theory of science and consequently of induction.

Plato [says Mill] gave great prominence to the doctrine that all individual and sensible objects, being in a perpetual process of change, never being but always becoming, there could be no knowledge in any true sense of the term, of them but only of certain archetypes or forms; which forms are the attributes in their completeness, an imperfect semblance of which we recognize in the best objects of sense. These forms had, according to him, a separate existence of their own, quite apart from sense. These were the only real Entia, or being; the world of sense was something halfway between Entity and Non-Entity.[1]

And this is a distinction which Mill faithfully observes throughout his account of the deductive method.

4. This is not, however, the case with his theory of the experimental methods. Here he assumes not only that all particulars are expressions of universals but also that all particulars may be immediately known as such. On the basis of these assumptions he reduces the problem of induction to the formal one of determining what universals in one particular are related to what universals in another particular; and it is this problem that he solves (or attempts to solve) by means of his canons of induction. But while the first of these assumptions is consistent with Mill's cosmological doctrine, the second is not. It is impossible, according to that doctrine,

[1] *Dissertations*, iv. 202 (condensed).

for the underlying forces of nature ever to become objects of sense. All that they can do is to produce upon the surface of experience objects of sense which are very different from themselves.

So far as Mill's theory of the experimental methods is concerned, this difficulty makes itself felt more particularly in regard to the term *cause* which he represents (and has to represent) sometimes as the phenomenal antecedent of an event and sometimes as the underlying tendency, or set of tendencies, which explains it. But the difficulty itself is a thoroughly general one. Nor is it easy to understand how Mill came to overlook it; for it is not only an obvious corollary from his general principles; it is also a corollary which on other occasions, as in his theory of experience, he is extremely anxious to emphasize under the heading of the *Relativity of Knowledge*.

5. Mill postulates an abiding reality of forces beneath the flux of appearances so as to provide objects of which we can have certain and systematic knowledge. Then in order to square this conception with the only body of certain and systematic knowledge with which he was acquainted he indentifies the relation of reality and appearance with the relation of cause and effect. But now, passing from cosmology to epistemology, he has to give an account of the occurrence of knowledge in these terms. And the only possible conclusion that he can come to is that we can never know the reality as it is in itself but only as the hidden cause of the impressions which it produces in us.

The inmost nature or essence of a thing [he says] is apt to be regarded as something unknown which if we knew it would explain and account for all the phenomena which the thing exhibits to us. But this unknown something is a supposition without evidence. . . . Moreover if there were such a central property it could not answer the idea of an inmost notion; for if knowable by any intelligence it must like other properties be relative to the intelligence which knows it; that is, it must solely consist in producing in that intelligence some specifically definite state of consciousness; for this is the only idea we have of knowing; the only sense in which the verb *to know* means anything.[1]

Hence at this stage of his argument, Mill's assertion of a reality underlying appearances becomes tinged with a certain air of doubt. Since there is no reason on his premises why the doubt should not grow, it does grow. Consequently the only things of whose existence Mill is finally sure are appearances whose characteristics are completely different from those of the reality which he began by postulating. For that reality consisted of material forces like the force of gravity, while the appearances (being the effects of the forces upon our minds) are mental impressions. And then, again, the forces were universals while their knowable results (being the effects of the exertion of the forces on this occasion and that) are particular events.

6. I conceive, therefore, that it is not because of any accidental illogicality in Mill's mind but because of the inherent logic of his position that he continually oscillates between the doctrines of realism and of nominalism. The issue, for instance, with which he is faced in regard to causation is properly described as one between realism and nominalism. So far as Mill finds the whole meaning of causation in the particular sequences which appear on the surface of experience, he gives a nominalist interpretation of it. So far as he regards these sequences as the manifestation of underlying tendencies which do not themselves appear upon the surface of experience, he gives a realist interpretation of it.

His realism, again, finds expression in the attributive view of propositions which is implied by his doctrine of scientific explanation, his nominalism in the class view of propositions which implies the theory of the syllogism usually associated with his name. But in point of fact there is scarcely any topic

---

[1] *Examination of Hamilton*, p. 14.

discussed in the *Logic* regarding which he does not, at some time or other, endorse both the nominalist and the realist views. Thus he holds not only that syllogistic reasoning must be interpreted as inference from particulars to particulars, but also that it must be regarded as indicating the applicability to a particular case of a universal connexion (or disconnexion) of attributes. And although no doubt Mill rather prided himself upon his discovery of the former interpretation, the latter also bulks quite large in his *Logic*.

Moreover, as a politician, Mill found it extremely convenient to be able to oscillate in this way between the realist and the nominalist points of view. He is a realist, for all his disclaimers, so long as he is concerned with providing a basis for the dogmatic side of radicalism. He becomes a nominalist as soon as he has to allow for its critical and destructive side.

Nevertheless it would scarcely be correct to say that Mill sometimes endorses this rationalist or realist theory of knowledge and sometimes an experientialist or nominalist one. In the last resort he must be regarded as primarily a rationalist; for the paradoxical feature of Mill's position (and I would add of the positions of all the other exponents of the way of ideas with the possible exception of Berkeley) is that his rationalism appears nowhere more plainly than in the way in which he justifies and defines his appeals to experience.

7. The experience to which Mill appeals is never experience as we have it here and now, but always 'analysed experience'; that is, experience in which a firm distinction is drawn between its original and its acquired elements. Moreover, Mill is convinced from the beginning that he knows exactly how this distinction is to be drawn. He never dreams of approaching the problem in a simple-minded, unsophisticated fashion by describing mental phenomena as he finds them, noting their constant and variable features, the order of their appearance and so on, and gradually working back to

hypotheses about how they began and how they subsequently developed. On the contrary, he begins by assuming that mental phenomena can only have developed in one way——by aggregation or composition through the laws of association. Consequently he emphatically repudiates the suggestion that we have anything to learn from the unprejudiced study of our present states of consciousness and maintains instead, with Locke, that we must begin by studying the origin of our ideas.

Being unable [he says] to examine the actual contents of our consciousness until our earliest, which are necessarily our most firmly knit associations, are fully formed, we cannot study the original elements of mind in the facts of our present consciousness. These original elements can only come to light as residual phenomena by a previous study of the mental elements which are confessedly not original.[1]

But, in fact, Mill is as guiltless as Locke of any indecision about these original elements of our consciousness either. He never attempts to bring them to light as residual phenomena. He simply assumes, without even defining what he means by the term, that they are 'sensations'.

8. Thus Mill was never in any doubt that by the aid of these twin concepts of sensation and association, he and his predecessors had succeeded in giving to psychology its 'final scientific form'. He no more doubted this than he doubted that Newton had succeeded in giving physics its final scientific form by the aid of the law of gravitation; and this indeed is a simile of which both Mill and his predecessors are particularly fond. 'Here', says Hume of the association of ideas, 'is a kind of *Attraction* which in the mental world will be found to have as extraordinary effects as in the material.' 'Hardly anything universal can be affirmed in psychology', says Mill, 'except the laws of association.' They, he repeats, are to psychology 'what the law of gravitation is to astronomy'.

[1] *Examination of Hamilton*, pp. 178 f.

Nor is it difficult to discover the considerations that moved Mill to make these assumptions regarding the nature of experience. An acceptable science of mind, according to his way of thinking, has to satisfy two basic requirements. In regard to its form, it must be similar to the received physical sciences; in regard to its content, it must be continuous with them. The first of these requirements defines the problem of psychology for him.[1] The second provides the essential clue for the solution of the problem; for it is a fundamental though unacknowledged principle of his that nothing is to be admitted as ultimate in psychology which is not immediately explicable in terms of physics and physiology. Thus he admitted sensations as the ultimate elements of experience because he could point to processes in the sense organs in which they originated. He admitted laws of association as the ultimate bonds of connexion between sensations and ideas, and between ideas and ideas, because he believed in the plasticity of the nervous system. But as for the rest, as he could find no physiological basis for any other alleged psychical elements or laws, he held that they must be explained away as mere appearances.

Something further will be said about Mill's psychology and epistemology in Chapter X. In the next two chapters I shall consider the bearing of his doctrine of the relativity of knowledge on his theories of the syllogism and of mathematics.

---

[1] Mill defines his father's psychology, which is substantially the same as his own, as 'an attempt to reach the simplest elements which by their combination generate the manifold complexity of our mental states, and to assign the laws of those elements, and the elementary laws of their combination, from which laws, the subordinate ones which govern the compound states are consequences and corollaries'. *Analysis of Mind*, vol. 1, Preface, p. x.

VIII

THEORIES OF THE SYLLOGISM

1. Of all the doctrines advanced or endorsed by Mill none has engendered more heat and less light than his theory of the syllogism; and for this state of affairs Mill's critics, I believe, are fully as much to blame as Mill himself. On the one hand, they have generally concentrated their attention far too exclusively on Mill's actual account of the syllogism to the detriment of those wider considerations from which he derived it. (Venn and Bain are outstanding exceptions to the run of Mill's critics in this respect.) On the other hand, they have failed to notice that the nominalist theory of the syllogism usually associated with Mill's name is not the only theory which he actually asserts. Or if they have noticed this odd and interesting fact, they have obscured its significance by making use of it merely for polemical purposes—by playing off one statement of Mill's against another.

In this chapter I shall endeavour to obtain some positive result from Mill's discussion of the syllogism by stressing these neglected points; in the following chapter—on Mill's theory of mathematics—I hope to amplify this result. Thus it is a question here, as I see it, of tracing the connexion between Mill's general conception of logic, his theory of the import of propositions, and his nominalist theory of the syllogism. And then again it is a question of accounting for the fact that Mill does not always endorse a nominalist theory of the syllogism. Indeed on the evidence of all his statements in the *Logic* (including what he has to say about terms and propositions as well as about reasoning) there are almost as good grounds for crediting him with a realist as with a nominalist theory of the syllogism. There are other passages, moreover, in which he appears to endorse the traditional formalist theory. And these three theories—the formalist, the realist, and the nominalist—seem to be the only ones that can be offered on this subject.

The Formalist Theory

2. Like some contemporary scholars, Bacon thought of the syllogistic logic as a development of Aristotle's attempt to regularize the sort of disputations that are recorded in Plato's dialogues. In this context, moreover, he considered that the syllogism had an intelligible function as a way of settling a difference of opinion about some propositions by discovering other propositions to which both parties could agree and from which the disputed proposition (or its contradictory) could be inferred. If, however, logic is regarded as a means, not of seeking agreement among disputants, but of discovering the truth about things, then it is not at all easy, he points out, to see what purpose can be served by the syllogism. As its conclusiveness depends upon agreement about propositions, so agreement about propositions depends upon agreement about the concepts used in them. But concepts refer to things and the great need, from Bacon's point of view, is that they should correctly refer to things.

Thus it is not surprising that when Bacon contemplated the possibility of a logic concerned with 'the discovery not of what agrees with principles but of principles themselves', he should have rejected the help of the syllogism. He was engaged in a quest for certainty which required him, as it required Descartes, to make a completely fresh start unhindered by the efforts of previous thinkers. Where Descartes sought within his own reason for propositions (like the *Cogito ergo sum*) which asserted, and hence guaranteed themselves, Bacon called rather for the discovery of brute facts untainted by reason. But Aristotle, in Bacon's opinion at least, had not pretended to dig so deep in his logic; he was concerned only that men should make the best use of the knowledge they already had without inquiring into its ultimate evidence; hence Bacon was unable to make any use of his teaching.

Nevertheless Bacon did not deny the validity of the Aristotelian logic within its own sphere, nor did he propose to incorporate it into his new logic. He suggested rather that as their aims were different—the one attempting 'to subdue an opponent in disputation, the other to command nature in action'—the two logics should be regarded as two independent 'streams and dispensations of knowledge'.[1] To all appearances he says this as much from conviction as from policy. And Mill sometimes says exactly the same thing.

3. In his *Examination of Hamilton* (which contains his maturest reflections on this subject) Mill argues that as logic is concerned with valid thinking, and as the end of thinking is *truth*, we can never satisfy ourselves that the end has been attained 'by looking merely at the relation of one part of a train of thought to another'. Nevertheless he does concede that we may sometimes discover that a proposition is *false* without ascending to the original sources of our knowledge. A concept or judgement, for example, may involve a contradiction; or a syllogism may have passed from premisses to conclusion through an ambiguous term. Consequently he is quite prepared to segregate from the remainder of the theory of the investigation of truth as 'much of it as does not require any reference to the original sufficiency of the groundwork of facts or the correctness of their interpretation'. Thus in Mill's view at this time there are two logics to be distinguished—the 'logic of consistency' or 'formal logic' which scrutinizes the processes by which truths are known through the medium of other truths and the 'logic of truth' which includes also the consideration of the premisses by which first truths are known. (Mill's followers sometimes speak of them as 'conceptualist' and 'material' logic respectively.) Consequently Mill like

---

[1] Bacon, *Instauratio Magna*, Distributio Operis; *Novum Organum*, Aph. 14, 36, Praefatio.

Bacon is able on occasion to give an account of the reasoning process which is completely in line with the traditional theory of the syllogism.[1]

'Particulars alone', Mill says for example, 'are capable of being subjected to observation; and all knowledge which is derived from observation begins, therefore, of necessity in particulars; but our knowledge may in cases of certain descriptions be conceived as coming to us from other sources than observation.' It may, for example, come from testimony, as when a theological doctrine is accepted on the authority of scripture; or, again, it may come by way of command rather than assertion, as when a government requires all men to do something or other. 'In both these cases', Mill admits, 'the generalities are the original data and the particulars are elicited from them by a process which correctly resolves itself into a series of syllogisms.' There is also, as he subsequently points out, a further case of a similar sort in which we assume but do not assert the truth of certain propositions simply in order to trace their consequences; and here again he is careful to leave us in no doubt about his opinion of the legitimacy of this procedure. 'It is, of course,' he says, 'quite as practicable to arrive at new conclusions from facts assumed as from facts observed; from fictitious as from real inductions.'[2]

In certain cases, then, as when the theologian argues from scripture, the lawyer from law, or the scientist from hypotheses, Mill is fully prepared to agree that it is pointless, inexpedient, or downright impossible to reduce general propositions to collections of particular facts. In these cases, consequently, he is fully prepared also to admit the validity of syllogistic reasoning in its traditional form. But these, it may be contended, are precisely the sort of cases that the syllogistic logician who knows his business has in mind all along. Nor is it difficult to furnish an interpretation of the Socrates argument along these lines. Imagine a person in Socrates'

---

[1] *Examination of Hamilton*, pp. 470 ff.   [2] *Logic*, ii. 3. 4; ii. 6. 4.

lifetime genuinely doubtful about his mortality and then imagine another person anxious, for some reason, to convince him about it. His efforts in these circumstances may well take the form of an examination—'I suppose you believe that Socrates is a man? You also believe that all men are mortal, don't you? Then you must believe that Socrates is mortal.' And so far as we are all open to such appeals to consistency (and are right to be open to them) we are bound, I take it, to admit that the interlocutor has made out his case.

4. Mill's usual position regarding the nature of logic, and consequently of the syllogism, is, however, completely different. The full title of his book is *A System of Logic—Ratiocinative and Inductive*, and he describes it in the preface as 'an attempt not to supersede, but to embody and sytematize, the best ideas which have been either promulgated on its subject by speculative writers, or conformed to by accurate thinkers in their scientific enquiries'. Hence Mill makes no pretence of giving to the world a new theory of the intellectual operations; and indeed he considers that in the existing state of science there would be a strong presumption against anyone who did. But he does admit that a certain amount of original speculation was required 'to cement together the detached fragments of a subject never yet treated as a whole'; and in doing so he hints at one of the most important characteristics of his treatment of it.

As he was concerned to give a connected account of the subject, he attempts to provide a foundation for ratiocination which will serve also for induction. Hence he was not content to allow the logic of consistency and the logic of truth to stand side by side as independent disciplines, but endeavoured to reduce the former to the latter. It was in these terms that Mill's purpose in the *Logic* was understood by those who were best acquainted with it and with him; thus Bain reports that 'it was considered by many—most emphatically by Grote—that Mill had introduced for the first time a unity into logic, had bridged the chasm that separated the inductive from syllogistic logic';[1] and it was in these terms also that Mill sometimes expressed his own convictions.

If thought [he says, for example] be anything more than a sportive exercise of the mind, its purpose is to enable us to know what can be known respecting the facts of the universe; its judgments and conclusions express, or are intended to express, some of these facts; and the connexion which formal logic, by its analysis of the reasoning process, points out between one proposition and another, exists only because there is a connexion between one objective truth and another, which makes it possible for us to know objective truths which have never been observed, in virtue of others which have. This possibility is an eternal mystery and stumbling block to formal logic. But what the logic of mere consistency cannot do, the logic of the ascertainment of truth, the philosophy of evidence in its larger acceptation, can. It is therefore alone competent to furnish a philosophical theory of reasoning.[2]

5. It is true that in spite of all Mill's efforts to bridge the chasm separating the inductive from the syllogistic logic, he still managed to leave a considerable gap between them. As regards the former, the opponents he had principally in mind were men like Macaulay who denied the possibility of making anything demonstrative out of induction and consequently cast doubt upon the feasibility of the utilitarian attempt to refashion political philosophy into social science. As regards the latter, he was mainly concerned to oppose the teaching of men like Whewell who held that the first principles of reasoning, in mathematics as in morals, were to be discovered by intuition as distinct from observation. I have therefore suggested in Chapter IV that we should find that Mill took his experientialism a good deal more seriously in Book II of his *Logic* than in Book III; I have also suggested that this

---

[1] Bain, *Dissertations*, p. 25.
[2] *Examination of Hamilton*, pp. 479 f. (condensed).

difference would lead to a considerable difference in his estimate of the possibilities of certain knowledge in the two places; and it is easy enough to confirm these suggestions by comparing his theories of induction and of the syllogism.

In his theory of induction Mill assumes that all particulars are expressions of universals; he also assumes (somewhat inconsistently) that all particulars may be immediately known as such; and on the basis of these assumptions he redefines the problem of induction as one of analysis rather than generalization. In his theory of the syllogism, on the other hand, Mill opposes the acceptance of the universal propositions that are usually supposed to be involved in all reasoning. In his view it is necessary to penetrate behind their façade of universality to the evidence upon which they rest. When we do so, he argues, we find nothing but particulars. Hence, as he concludes that all inference is from particulars to particulars, he allows us to conclude that all inference is uncertain; for the universals by which we pretend to connect particulars are themselves nothing but collections of particulars.

Thus while Mill's theory of induction is based (in intention at least) upon a realist theory of universals, his theory of reasoning is based upon a nominalist theory. Nor is there any possible way of softening the contrast between Mill's treatment of these two topics, so long, at least, as we understand by his theory of reasoning the nominalist theory of the syllogism that is usually associated with his name. But all the same it is not difficult, I believe, to explain how Mill came to make the transition from the one mode of treatment to the other. We have already had occasion to notice in connexion with Mill's theory of induction that his realism has an inherent tendency to contradict itself by developing into nominalism; and it is upon these lines also, I believe—that is, by presuming the dependence of his nominalism upon his realism— that we should attempt to account for Mill's puzzling recurrences, in his theory of reasoning, to a realist position.

Realist and Nominalist Theories

6. Two alternative views are commonly recognized regarding the nature of the matters of fact asserted in propositions. According to the nominalists, they are always in the last resort particulars, and any universals which appear to be asserted are reducible in some way to particulars. According to the realists, it is impossible to get behind the reference to universals, and it can be shown that the references to particulars also involve references to universals. These doctrines are sometimes called the class and attributive theories of propositions respectively; and they are associated with the fact that the terms of propositions, or at least the general terms, have two sorts of meaning or make two sorts of reference. The term *man*, for instance, *denotes* the class of men to which it applies but *connotes* the attributes which all men have in common; similarly the term *mortal* denotes everything that has died or is going to die, connotes the attribute mortality or liability to death; and generally speaking the connotation of a concrete general term is indicated by the corresponding abstract term—as *humanity* corresponds to *man*, and *mortality* to *mortal*; its denotation by the plural of the concrete term—*men* and *mortals*.

Now if the terms of the proposition, *All men are mortal*, are read in denotation, it will mean that the class of men is included in the class of mortals. If the terms are read in connotation, it will mean that the attribute humanity is constantly associated with the attribute mortality. Thus the decision between the class and the attributive views of the import of propositions depends upon whether classes are regarded as prior to attributes or *vice versa*; and it is remarkably easy to argue on either side. Classes, it may be held, depend on attributes because it is only by means of attributes that the various members of classes are what they are. On the other hand, it may be held that attributes are nothing but resemblances between the various members of classes and hence that the former depend for their existence upon the latter.

But although the decision between the class view and the attributive view of propositions turns on so fine a point, the consequences of the decision are far reaching. According to the class view, a general truth is nothing but an aggregate of particular truths, and therefore the singular proposition, *Socrates is mortal*, is included in the universal proposition, *All men are mortal*. It follows that we cannot without arguing in a circle adduce the universal proposition as evidence for the singular proposition. Hence, the syllogism on this view must be condemned as involving a *petitio principii*.[1] On the attributive view, however, the syllogism does not involve a *petitio principii*, because the assertion of the universal proposition does not include the assertion of any singular proposition. It merely asserts a connexion or disconnexion of attributes. Hence it may be true even although there are no singular propositions to be subsumed under it. It may be true even if there cannot possibly be any such singular propositions.

7. Now as between the class and the attributive views of the proposition, Mill begins by declaring unhesitatingly for the latter. The 'real meaning' of the name, *man*, he holds, consists in the attributes connoted and not in the individuals denoted by it; and similarly with the name, *mortal*. Hence when we say, *All men are mortal*, we are saying that 'the latter set of attributes constantly accompany the former set' and it is only as a consequence of this fact that the class of men is included in the class of mortals. Mill supports this view by

---

[1] At the same time the *dictum de omni et nullo* (which is the general axiom of the syllogism) must be condemned on a similar ground. This axiom asserts that whatever can be affirmed (or denied) of a class may be affirmed (or denied) of everything included in the class. But the obvious difficulty with this formula on the class view of propositions is, as Mill points out, that 'the class *is* nothing but the objects contained in it; and the *dictum de omni* merely amounts to the identical proposition, that whatever is true of certain objects is true of each of these objects'. *Logic*, ii. 2. 2.

arguing (with Plato), that 'if by the *meaning* of a general name are to be understood the things which it is the name of, no general name, except by accident, has a fixed meaning at all, or ever long retains the same meaning'. Hence coming to the syllogism he proposes an interpretation of it in line with this view. Every syllogism, he says, comes within the general formula—'Attribute A is a mark of attribute B; The given object has the mark A; Therefore it has the attribute B.' The general axiom of the syllogism is then. 'Whatever has any mark, has that which it is a mark of', or, in other words, *Nota notae est nota rei ipsius.* And this axiom, according to Mill at one stage of his argument, expresses with precision and force 'what is aimed at, and actually accomplished, in every case of the ascertainment of truth by ratiocination'.[1]

The amazing thing is, however, that having put forward this account of the syllogism, Mill immediately reopens the whole inquiry by asking how it must be interpreted in order that it may avoid the charge of begging the question. On the face of it, he has already answered this question by saying that the propositions composing it are to be read attributively, since the truth of the major premiss, on this interpretation, is quite independent of the truth of the conclusion. Why, then, does not Mill meet the charge of *petitio principii* by drawing attention to this? Why, instead, does he think it necessary to propose the revolutionary doctrine that in the last resort all inference is from particulars to particulars, and never, as the theory of the syllogism assumes, from universals to particulars?

8. The answer is, I think, that, as on so many other occasions, Mill wants to have it both ways. The attributive view of propositions fits in very well with the abstract and metaphysical account of science commonly given by the utilitarians. It is therefore completely in line with the theory of scientific explanation that Mill gives in Book III and assumes

[1] Ibid. i. 5. 2 to 4; ii. 2. 3 and 4.

in Book VI of his *Logic*. But while he wishes to hold that everything that happens in the universe is explicable by reference to underlying laws of nature which state connexions between attributes, that hold independently of the occurrence of particular events, he also wishes to deny that we can know anything which does not appear upon the surface of experience. He is, moreover, forced to this denial because of his doctrine of the relativity of knowledge which is an inescapable implication of his metaphysical and abstract conception of science.

Thus the realist theory of universals, which is the proper correlative of the attributive theory of propositions is condemned on the ground that it personifies abstractions and leads to mysticism. With the rejection of realism comes the assumption of nominalism and consequently of the class theory of propositions. This implies that 'from a general principle we cannot infer any particulars but those which the principle itself assumes as known'. And, then, having reached this point Mill has no alternative (on his usual view of logic at least) but to assert the theory of the syllogism which is usually associated with his name. That is: 'All inference is from particulars to particulars. General propositions are merely registers of such inferences already made, and short formulae for making more: The major premiss of the syllogism, consequently, is a formula of this description; and the conclusion is not an inference drawn *from* the formula, but an inference drawn *according to* the formula: the real logical antecedent or premiss being the particular facts from which the general proposition was collected by induction.'[1]

Criticism of the Nominalist Theory

9. Mill's contemporaries were so strongly impressed by the close connexion between this doctrine of the syllogism and the avowed and notorious tenets of nominalism that they

[1] *Logic,* ii. 3. 4.

were sometimes inclined to give him little credit for it. Martineau described it as 'among the standing marks of what is called the empirical philosophy'. Bain thought of it as growing out of 'the sound view of general names and propositions, which any thoroughgoing nominalist would be likely to bring to light'. Even Herschel, who agreed with it, doubted whether it should be regarded as a discovery on the ground that Mill was 'only following out more emphatically the views originally taken by Berkeley on the subject'. Hence it is scarcely surprising that Mill should have been at some pains to insist upon the novelty of his doctrine.[1]

Mill's contemporaries were, however, certainly correct on this historical point. Sketching the genesis of his views regarding the syllogism, Mill relates in the *Autobiography* how he had puzzled himself with the great paradox of the discovery of new truths by general reasoning. 'As to the fact', he thought, 'there could be no doubt. As little could it be doubted that all reasoning is resolvable into syllogisms, and that in every syllogism the conclusion is actually contained or implied in the premisses.' But the question then arose, how being so contained or implied it could be a new truth? And failing to find any satisfactory answer to this question in the textbooks, Mill was completely at a loss until he came upon an idea in Dugald Stewart which seemed to provide a key to the problem.[2]

Now this idea of Stewart's (which is also an idea of Locke's) is that although our proofs in mathematics depend upon axioms, it is by no means necessary to the conclusiveness of the proofs that the axioms should be 'expressly adverted to'. When it is inferred, for example, that the line *AB* is equal to the line *CD* because each of them is equal to *EF*, the most uncultivated person, it is argued by Stewart, would assent to the inference as soon as he understood it, even if

[1] Martineau, *Essays*, iii. 525; Bain, *Dissertations*, p. 23; Herschel, *Essays*, p. 367; Mill, *Logic*, ii. 3. 8.   [2] *Autobiography*, p. 153.

he had never heard of the general truth, that things which are equal to the same thing are equal to each other. Hence Stewart concludes that the axioms of geometry are not, like the definitions, principles *from which* we reason but rather principles *according to which* we reason.[1] But Mill, generalizing Stewart's argument, concludes rather that we do not reason *from* general principles at all but only *according* to them.

Thus by Mill's own admission, the leading idea of his theory of the syllogism was borrowed from Stewart and Stewart himself acknowledges that he had borrowed it from Locke. Nor can Mill even claim the credit, such as it is, of having been the first to generalize the idea, since he had been preceded in this by Berkeley. It is true, as Mill points out, that Berkeley makes no actual reference to the syllogism—probably because it was already in sufficiently bad odour in his day. But it is also true, as Herschel suggests, that the interesting and important part of Berkeley's argument against abstract ideas consists of a theory of demonstrative reasoning which is identical with Mill's. It is to be noted, moreover, that both philosophers make use of exactly the same ambiguity in the key word—*particular*; and it is this ambiguity, I suggest, which is responsible for the curious mirage effect—Now you see it and now you don't—that the theory commonly produces.

10. 'Suppose', says Berkeley, 'a geometrician is demonstrating the method of cutting a line in two equal parts. He draws, for instance, a black line of an inch in length; this which in itself is a particular line, is nevertheless *with respect to its signification* general; since, as it is there used, it represents all particular lines whatsoever; so that what is demonstrated of it is demonstrated of all lines, or in other words, of a line in general.' What assumption, asks Mill, do we set out from to demonstrate by a diagram any of the properties of the

---

[1] Stewart, *Elements of the Philosophy of the Human Mind*, ii. 1. 1 and 2.

circle? 'Not', he answers, 'that in all circles the radii are equal, but only that they are so in the circle ABC.' Thus only one instance of the theory is demonstrated. But as the process by which this is done might be copied in any other instance *'which conforms to certain conditions'*, we are able to assert this indefinite multitude of truths in a single expression which is the general theorem.[1]

Now it may be argued against Berkeley and Mill that as a particular is nothing but a particular instance of a class, and as a class is only definable by a universal, it is impossible for us to refer to a particular without making some reference to a universal. Hence, it may be held that the doctrine that inference proceeds from particulars to particulars, independently of universals, is self-contradictory. This argument, however, scarcely seems tenable in view of the different ways in which we may refer to particulars. When we refer to them by means of demonstratives, like *this* or *that*, no universals at all are involved; and although it is by no means clear, indeed, that proper names, like *Socrates*, are demonstratives of exactly the same type (as Mill endeavoured to establish), it can hardly be maintained, either, that their use involves the assumption of universals in the way that is asserted in the objection.

Let us then restate the objection. It would seem that a broad distinction may be drawn between two quite different meanings of *a particular*. It may mean some particular thing pointed to, where no reference is made to its membership of a class or, at any rate, where no stress is laid upon its class characteristics. Or it may mean some particular member of a class whose class characteristics are obvious enough to justify us in treating it as a typical member, that is as *any* member, of its class. The former meaning, it is plain, does not involve the reference to a universal of the sort objected to, the latter does.

[1] Berkeley, *Principles of Human Knowledge*, Introduction, sec. 12; Mill, *Logic*, ii. 3. 3.

Thus the question becomes: How is the term *particular* actually used by Berkeley and Mill? The answer is that they use it in both senses according to their convenience. The appearance of novelty in their doctrine is produced by an initial emphatic use of the term which suggests pointing; for example, a black line of an inch in length. The appearance of plausibility, however, depends entirely upon *this* particular being finally represented as *any* member of a class; that is, as a line in general. Hence in order to create the impression that their doctrine is both novel and plausible, Mill and Berkeley have to switch meanings in the course of their exposition of it; and this inevitably entails the admission, which they both make quite explicitly, that the whole trick of proving a theorem by means of a diagram lies in ignoring most of its characteristics.

11. Though the idea I have in view [says Berkeley], whilst I make the demonstration be for instance that of an isosceles rectangular triangle whose sides are of a determinate length, I may nevertheless be certain it extends to all other rectilinear triangles, of what sort or bigness soever. And that because neither the right angle, nor the equality, nor determinate length of the sides are at all concerned in the demonstration. It is true the diagram I have in view includes all these particulars; but then there is not the least mention made of them in the proof of the proposition. . . . And it must here be acknowledged that a man may *consider* a figure merely as triangular, without attending to the particular qualities of the angles or relations of the sides.[1]

Thus we now have Berkeley explicitly admitting that the sort of inference he has in view proceeds from generals rather than from particulars. The only point that he now seems to be making is that, in so far as a reference is necessarily made to diagrams in this sort of inference, its generality must be regarded, in some sense or other, as a generality *of* particulars. Even this point vanishes when Mill, developing

[1] Berkeley, op. cit., sect. 16.

Berkeley's argument to its logical conclusion, takes the final step of admitting that 'by dropping the use of diagrams and substituting, in the demonstration, general phrases for the letters of the alphabet, we might prove the general theorem directly'.[1]

Nevertheless there is a difference between the cases of Mill and of Berkeley in that on other occasions, in regard to other instances of inference, Mill baulks at making the transition from *some* particular to *any* particular which Berkeley effects so smoothly. Hence we may also learn from him what becomes of the doctrine that inference is from particulars to particulars under these circumstances.

This type of ratiocination [says Mill] does not claim, like the syllogism, to be conclusive from the mere form of the expression; nor can it possibly be so. That one proposition does or does not assert the very fact which was already asserted in another, may appear from the very form of the expression, that is, from the comparison of the language; but when the two propositions assert facts which are *bona fide* different, whether the one fact proves the other fact or not can never appear from the language but must depend on other considerations.

In other passages, moreover, Mill actually goes so far as to reduce inference, on this basis, to a free play of association, in regard to which it would be absurd to raise the question of validity at all. 'If reasoning', he says, for example, 'be from particulars to particulars, nothing is required to render reasoning possible, except senses and association; senses to perceive that two facts are conjoined; association as the law, by which one of these two facts raises up the idea of the other.'[2]

Conclusion

12. It does not, then, appear difficult to arrive at a reasonable opinion regarding the theory that inference always proceeds from particulars to particulars. According to this theory

[1] *Logic*, ii. 3. 3.   [2] Ibid. ii. 3. 7; iv. 3. 2.

any argument will take the following form: 'Certain individuals have a given attribute; an individual or individuals resemble the former in certain other attributes; therefore they resemble them also in the given attribute.' Thus the Socrates syllogism, 'cut down to as much as is really known by direct evidence', will read—'My father and my father's father and an indefinite number of other persons have died; Socrates resembles these persons in certain respects; Therefore he will also resemble them in this.'[1] But it is not a convincing interpretation. It has the advantage of not begging the question; it has the further advantage of not assuming the existence of anything which does not appear upon the surface of experience; but it suffers from what may well be regarded as the fatal defect, in an interpretation of inference, of representing every inference as inconclusive.

The argument can be conclusive only if it is assumed that there is a constant connexion between the given attribute of certain individuals and the inferred attribute, that is, between humanity and mortality. But to assume that is to deny this reading of the syllogism; for although, no doubt, it is interesting and important *in psychology* to distinguish between the assumptions *from* which and those *according to* which we reason, that distinction can have no standing in logic. It is quite immaterial to the logician whether the proposition, *Humanity is a mark of mortality*, is 'expressly adverted to' by the reasoner. The only material question is whether the reasoner needs to assume this proposition in order to arrive at his conclusion. Seeing that he does, it has to be regarded as a premiss of his reasoning, if the reasoning is to be represented as conclusive. Hence, strictly interpreted, the theory that inference always proceeds from particulars to particulars amounts to a denial of its possibility. In order, then, to save inference both Berkeley and Mill have usually interpreted the theory loosely; in which case it rapidly becomes indis-

[1] *Logic.* ii. 3. 6.

tinguishable from the orthodox theory that inference proceeds from universals to particulars.

13. But all the same this cannot be regarded as the end of the matter, as most of Mill's critics seem to assume. Granted that Mill's theory of syllogism is untenable, his difficulty regarding it has still to be met. Nor is it sufficient to say that, somehow or other, the traditional theory must be reinstated. The question remains: How is it to be reinstated?

Consider, for example, Jevons's comments on Mill.

> We can only argue from the past to the future [he says] on the general principle that what is true of a thing will be true of a thing will be true of the like. So far as one object or event differs from another, all inference is impossible; particulars, as particulars, can no more make an inference than grains of sand can make a rope. We must always rise to something that is general or the same in the cases, and assuming that sameness to be extended to new cases we learn their nature.[1]

Scarcely anybody would take exception to these sentiments. The only difficulty is that they leave all the hard questions unanswered. What, for example, is the status of this *something* common to all the particular cases? How exactly do we *rise* to it from the contemplation of the particulars? How do we know that the other party has risen to it, when he points a syllogism at us? Unless we have answers to these questions, which Jevons had not, we cannot claim to have seen through the problem of the syllogism; and although Mill's solution of the problem is certainly unsatisfactory we may still, I think, learn from him something about the conditions governing a satisfactory solution.

14. According to the traditional logic, a syllogism is to be regarded as part of a peculiar sort of conversation which a man may carry on with another man or with himself.[2] The

---

[1] Jevons, *Principles of Science*, 3rd ed., p. 228.

[2] The assumption here is that it is the dialectical syllogism which is fundamental in Aristotle's logic and that the apodeictic syllogism was added as an afterthought. For a defence of this assumption see Kapp, *Greek Foundations of Traditional Logic*.

elements of the conversation are propositions, some of which are universal, some particular. Elements of both kinds are given and are recognizable by their forms. Certain relations among propositions—of equivalence, of subsumption, and of contradiction—are also given and are also formally recognizable. The purpose of the conversation is to demonstrate the consistency or inconsistency of a given set of propositions by means of their formal relations. Hence the validity of the process depends directly on the validity of the traditional theory regarding the formal analysis of propositions.

This part of reasoning [as Bain puts it] is found to make a study of itself; and its expounders are not to be held as denying the necessity of looking to the matter on the proper occasion. If logicians have been too exclusively occupied with this formal condition of sound inference, that is their infirmity. Any formalist that chooses to state his position guardedly could, in answer to the charge of *petitio principii* retort upon Mill the equally grave charge of *ignoratio elenchi*.[1]

15. The trouble is, however, that although Mill endorses the traditional formal analysis of propositions readily enough,[2] his general conception of logic forbade him to take it sufficiently seriously. The principal reason, in his opinion, why logic had made such inconsiderable progress in the previous two centuries was the notion 'that what is of primary im-

[1] Bain, *Dissertations*, pp. 21 ff.
[2] A proposition, Mill says, is 'a discourse in which something is affirmed or denied of something'. Thus in the proposition *Gold is yellow*, the quality yellow is affirmed of the substance gold; in the proposition *Franklin was not born in England*, the fact of being born in England is denied of the name Franklin. The predicate is the name of that which is affirmed or denied; the subject is the name of that of which something is affirmed or denied; the copula is the sign indicating that there is an affirmation or denial. Moreover, while this analysis applies in the first instance only to categorical propositions, Mill also holds that all propositions may be stated in this categorical form; disjunctive propositions being immediately reducible to hypotheticals and hypotheticals to categoricals. *Logic*, i. 4. 1 and 3.

portance to the logician in a proposition is the relation between the two *ideas* corresponding to the subject and predicate'. The result, he holds, was that what had been done
for the advancement of the subject since this view came into
vogue had been the work, not of professed logicians, but of
scientists 'in whose methods of investigation many principles
of logic not previously thought of have successively come
forth into light'. Consequently he proposed to remedy the
situation by insisting that, as a logician, he was only interested
in the facts asserted in propositions. He admits, indeed, that
propositions also involve ideas of facts and acts of believing
or judging; but ideas, he argues, are 'mental representations'
or 'mental conceptions'—'facts in my mental history'—which
are essential to judgement but form no part of what is judged;
and acts of judgement, again, are states of mind whose consideration belongs not to logic but to 'another science', meaning psychology.[1]

Thus as a result of Mill's scientific approach to logic he was
led, as he puts it, to take an extremely 'objective' view of propositions as against the 'conceptualist' or 'subjective' view of
the older logicians. Consequently, holding this view, he was
unable to attach much importance either to the traditional
analysis of propositions or to the formal theory of inference
which is based upon it. For if the import of propositions is to
be found exclusively in the matters of fact asserted by them,
it will follow, as Mill maintains, that 'the connection which
formal logic points out between one proposition and another
exists only because there is a connection between one objective truth and another'. Hence from this point onwards, the
important question for Mill is whether universals are to be
admitted among these objective truths or not. Since he
finally decides (and has to decide on his cosmological principles) that the only truths which we are capable of knowing
are particulars, he has also to decide (like Berkeley and Hume)

---

[1] Ibid. i. 5. 1.

that all inference must be regarded as proceeding from particulars to particulars, despite the fact that we can never perceive any connexion between them.

16. I conclude, then, in the first place that Mill's nominalist theory of the syllogism is the inevitable consequence of two other theories: (i) that the import of propositions is reducible entirely to the facts which they are about; (ii) that in the last resort these facts consist entirely of particulars. Hence I conclude in the second place that there are two, and only two, alternatives to this theory of the syllogism. Asserting (i) but denying (ii) we may hold, with the realists, that the facts referred to in propositions comprise universals as well as particulars. Denying (i) and ignoring (ii) we may hold, with the formalists, that the forms of propositions provide an adequate basis for a theory of inference independently of their matter. Thus granting that Mill's nominalist theory of the syllogism is unsatisfactory the question now arises: By which of these other theories is it to be replaced?

The great advantage of the formalist theory is that it requires no cosmological assumptions from the logician. It merely requires him, as Venn puts it, 'to start at any moment from our present standing point, or at most a step behind this, and to offer an account of our beliefs over this limited range'.[1] With this great advantage, however, the formalist theory has a corresponding disadvantage. It provides a set of formulae by which you can infallibly demonstrate that *if* a man (who may be yourself) holds certain beliefs, *then* he ought to hold certain other beliefs. But it provides (and can provide) no formula by which you can induce a man to assert the conclusions simply. In order to do that you have somehow to assure your man that there really is something in the fact which answers to the premisses; and when these facts are universal propositions there is, I believe, nothing for it but to assert the existence of corresponding universal facts.

[1] Venn, *Empirical Logic*, pp. 381 f.

Thus I conclude in the third place that while the formalist theory of the syllogism is tenable up to a certain point (which is capable of precise definition), it has to be replaced beyond that point by the realist theory.

It should be noted finally that this is a conclusion which becomes of considerable importance when we pass from the discussion of the syllogism to the discussion of mathematics. For in dealing with mathematics we are, or should be, concerned not only with the fact that certain conclusions follow from certain premises, but also with the further fact that, in a great many cases, the conclusions and therefore presumably the premises (or at least something very like them) are applicable to the real world. It is beside the point to object that the men who originally formulated the premises and drew the conclusions were not interested in the applications. The applications remain; and while they remain it is difficult to be satisfied with a theory of mathematics (like that of Bertrand Russell or Dugald Stewart) which tells us to forget about them. Thus it appears to me that those considerations regarding the ultimate material import of propositions which may be rejected as irrelevant to the discussion of the syllogism, from the formalist point of view, must be admitted as relevant to the discussion of mathematics. Although, moreover, it is not the easiest thing in the world to determine the conclusions at which Mill finally arrived on this topic, there are grounds for believing that on the whole he favoured a realist theory in line with the basic assumptions of his theory of induction.

DEBATE ON MATHEMATICS

1. I F we are to judge by his *Autobiography* we can have little doubt regarding Mill's attitude to mathematics. He believed that the great intellectual support of false doctrines and bad institutions was 'the theory that truths external to the mind may be known by intuition or consciousness independently of observation and experience'. He also believed that the great strength of this theory lay in 'the appeal which it is accustomed to make to the evidence of mathematics and of the cognate branches of physical science'. Hence in dealing with mathematics he was principally concerned, as he tells us, to meet the intuitive philosophers on their own ground by giving 'an explanation of the peculiar certainty of mathematics in terms of experience and association'; and, working on the reasonable assumption that a man may be expected to understand his own theories, most of Mill's critics have accepted this assurance and have judged him accordingly.[1]

When, however, we examine what Mill actually says about mathematics we find that his position is not nearly so unambiguous as he would have us believe; for while he does, indeed, devote considerable space to an attack on Whewell's intuitionist theory he leaves us in considerable doubt about his own. (i) Sometimes, it is true, he does give a straightforward account of mathematics in terms of experience.

Every theorem in geometry [he says, for example] is a law of external nature and might have been ascertained by generalizing from observation and experiment, which in this case resolve themselves into comparison and measurement. But it was found practicable and, being practicable, was desirable to deduce these truths by ratiocination from a small number of general laws of

[1] *Autobiography*, p. 191.

nature, the certainty and universality of which are obvious to the most careless observer.

(ii) At other times, however, he gives a very different account.

When it is affirmed that the conclusions of geometry are necessary truths [he also says in the *Logic*], the necessity consists in reality only in this, that they correctly follow from the suppositions from which they are deduced. These suppositions are so far from being necessary, that they are not even true; they purposely depart, more or less widely, from the truth. The only sense in which necessity can be ascribed to the conclusions of any scientific investigation, is that of legitimately following from some assumption, which, by the conditions of the inquiry, is not to be questioned.

(iii) If, moreover, we look beyond the *Logic* to what Mill says in his later years, we find yet another account of mathematics, in which he departs so far from the experiential theory as to represent the existence of mathematics as the prime exemplification of 'the fact that there actually is a road to truth by means of reasoning' as distinct from observation. He explains this by telling us that 'while the laws of Number underlie the laws of Extension, and these two underlie the laws of Force, so do the laws of Force underlie all the other laws of the material universe'. Subsequently he goes on to state or suggest a theory of mathematics which is much more in line with the basic assumptions of his theory of induction.[1]

2. Thus besides the experiential theory which he promised us, Mill also presents us with two other theories of mathematics; and his critics have not failed to draw attention to the discrepancies between them and the experiential theory. According to one of these theories, mathematics simply traces the consequences of certain hypotheses the truth of which 'by the conditions of the enquiry is not to be questioned'; according to the other, mathematics is concerned to elucidate

---

[1] *Logic*, iii. 24. 6; ii. 5. 1; *St. Andrews Address* (1867), p. 48; *Examination of Hamilton* (1865), p. 619.

the principles of 'abstract number and extension' which somehow 'underlie' the particular facts which we experience.

But while the critics are certainly right about the inconsistencies between Mill's various statements regarding mathematics, they are, I believe, wrong about the reasons they give for them. They usually suggest, as they do also in regard to Mill's various statements about the syllogism, that, being of an open-minded but illogical turn of mind, he has made concessions to his intuitionist opponents without perceiving how fatal they were to his own theory. In fact, however, the statements made by Mill which are inconsistent with an experiential theory of mathematics amount to a good deal more than concessions. They constitute two complete alternative theories which, to all appearances, play as large a part in Mill's thinking as the experiential theory itself. It is a complete mistake, moreover, to regard either of them as representing any approach to the intuitionist theory. They are as distinct from that as they are from each other.

It is much more to the point, I believe, to observe that the three theories of mathematics between which Mill hesitates are identical with the three theories that were noticed in connexion with the syllogism. (i) is the nominalist theory; (ii) is the traditional formalist theory; (iii) is the realist theory. But it is also necessary to take account of the state of philosophical thinking in England at this time since Mill scarcely makes a single statement about mathematics without referring to some contemporary or other.

Now so far as the nature of mathematics was under consideration in England at this time it was the subject of a three-cornered debate between intuitionists like Whewell, who had derived his theory from Kant; the followers of Dugald Stewart, who had derived his from Locke; and experientialists like Herschel who could claim the concurrence of certain other scientists. (There were no exponents of realism.) If, then, we regard Mill, as I think we must, as

continuing (and confusing) this debate, most of his statements about mathematics become intelligible enough provided that we allow for the extraordinary readiness with
which he changed sides; and tedious though it may be to
trace Mill through all his twists and turns, it is the only way
I believe to understand the considerations that really weighed
with him on this subject. In the first round of the debate,
Mill combines with Whewell to oppose Stewart's hypothetical
or formalist theory; in the second, he asserts the experiential
theory in opposition to Whewell; in the third, he endeavours
to meet a difficulty in the experiential theory by combining
it with the hypothetical theory; in the fourth, he abandons
them both for a realist theory.

3. The peculiar certainty that distinguishes mathematics
from other sciences arises, according to Dugald Stewart,
from a single circumstance: 'Whereas in all other sciences
the propositions which we attempt to establish express facts
real or supposed, in mathematics the propositions which we
demonstrate only assert a connection between certain suppositions and certain consequences.' Hence if we reason
correctly in mathematics from our original suppositions or
hypotheses, according to Stewart, 'nothing can be wanting to
complete the evidence of the result'. But in the other sciences,
even if every ambiguity of language is removed and every
step of our deductions is rigorously accurate, our conclusions must always be attended with more or less uncertainty
because they are 'ultimately founded on principles which
may or may not correspond exactly with the fact'.

This view evidently requires Stewart to draw a sharp
distinction between mathematics and physics. Consequently
he protests with equal vigour against regarding mathematics
as a branch of physics or physics as a branch of mathematics.
He is so firm about this that he finds it very difficult to explain
'the extensive and the various utility of mathematical knowledge in physical researches'; nor indeed is it at all clear that

he ever succeeded in thinking of it as anything but a 're-markable and singular coincidence'. It was also in the in-terests of this view that Stewart identified the first principles of geometry with the definitions of Euclid—to the exclusion of the axioms and postulates—since it is they which seem most definitely and deliberately to refrain from making any claim to truth.

In support of this contention Stewart then undertook to explain away the part played by axioms and postulates in Euclid's geometry. He maintained: (i) that all the postulates and some of the axioms are really disguised definitions; (ii) that some of the axioms are theorems deducible from the definitions; (iii) that the remaining axioms are not principles *from which* but rather principles *according to which* we reason. (It was this last method of disposing of axioms that suggested Mill's nominalist theory of the syllogism to him, but it plays no part in any of his theories of mathematics.) Instances of the axioms which Stewart disposed of by these three methods are: (i) magnitudes which coincide with one another are equal; (ii) all right angles are equal to one another; (iii) things which are equal to the same thing are equal to one another.[1]

4. Mill and Whewell, on the other hand, had in common a belief that all knowledge, and hence also mathematics, had a certain categorical character. They could not, therefore, regard it as consisting merely of floating ideas or as being founded on arbitrary hypotheses. In the long run, again, they were both bound to qualify the sharp distinction between pure and applied mathematics which Stewart had drawn. And it was on these grounds that they combined to criticize him.

Whewell argues that it is impossible to get rid of axioms by substituting definitions for them, as Stewart proposed, because every definition presupposes an axiom asserting the possibility

[1] Stewart, *Philosophy of the Human Mind,* part. ii, chaps. 1 and 4.

of the thing defined. Thus while Stewart demands the definitions which lie behind the axioms of geometry, Whewell
retorts by demanding the axioms which lie behind the definitions.[1] He goes on to maintain that when this demand is
satisfied the first principles of geometry cannot be regarded
as arbitrary, as Stewart maintained. And Mill arrived at much
the same conclusion by a slightly different route.

Propositions generally, according to Mill, assert facts, and
that is why they are true or false. But definitions do not
assert facts; they merely declare the meanings to be attached
to names; hence they cannot be true or false, nor can they be
the premisses of true or false conclusions. But the theorems
of geometry, according to Mill, are true; yet, according to
Euclid, they are deduced, in part, from definitions; hence it
would seem to follow that these definitions, at least, do more
than declare the meanings of names; and it had sometimes
been held (notably by Whately) that they are *real*, as distinct from *nominal*, definitions.

Mill replies that there *are* expressions, commonly passing
for definitions, which include in themselves more than the
bare declaration of the meaning of a term. 'But it is not correct
to call an expression of this sort a particular kind of definition.
Its difference from the other kind consists in this, that it is
not a definition but a definition and something more.' The
definition of a triangle, for example, 'obviously comprises
not one but two propositions perfectly distinguishable'. The
one is the *postulate*: 'There may exist a figure bounded by
three straight lines'; the other is the *definition*: 'This figure

[1] Suppose, for instance, that we attempt to replace the axiom, Two
straight lines cannot enclose a space, by the definition, A line is said to be
straight when two such lines cannot coincide in two points without
coinciding altogether. Before we lay this down as a definition, Whewell
contends, we need to be assured that it is possible for lines to have this
property. If this is not self-evident, we have no right to lay down the
definition. If it is self-evident, 'the simple and obvious method is to state
the property *as* a self-evident truth, that is, as an axiom.' *History of Scientific Ideas*, p. 113; *Mechanical Euclid*, p. 176.

may be termed a triangle.' Hence, as it is only the postulates which are susceptible to truth or falsity, Mill maintains that our reasonings in mathematics are based upon them.[1]

Thus *in the first round of the debate* Mill holds that our reasonings in mathematics 'are grounded on the matters of fact postulated in definitions and not on the definitions themselves'; and this is a conclusion which he gladly acknowledges that he has in common with Whewell. Beyond this point, however, their positions diverge very rapidly owing to a fundamental disagreement about the nature of the matters of fact which are postulated in these first principles. And it is upon this disagreement, which would have no meaning apart from their previous agreement, that Mill always lays most stress whenever he refers to mathematics.

5. To begin with, it was as plain to Whewell as to Kant that the axioms of geometry are conceived by us not only as true but as universally and necessarily true. He also maintains, like Kant, that they are necessarily true in two quite different senses. They are self-evident whenever we think about them. They are also indispensable whenever we think about space and therefore, according to Whewell, whenever we think about anything. 'We cannot conceive or perceive objects at all', he says, 'except as existing in space: we cannot conceive things in space without being led to consider them as related to straight lines, right angles and the like; and we cannot contemplate these relations distinctly without assuming those properties of straight lines and the like which are the basis of our geometry.'

But if this is the case, Whewell goes on, our knowledge of these properties cannot possibly be derived from experience. 'Experience', he points out, 'must always consist of a limited number of observations; and however numerous these may be, they can show nothing with regard to the infinite number of cases in which the experiment has not been made.' Ex-

---

[1] *Logic*, i. 8. 5 and 6.

perience, he holds again, cannot offer the slightest ground for the necessity of a proposition, since it will not enable us to detect 'any internal bond which indivisibly connects the future with the past, the possible with the real'. Hence, for his part, Whewell prefers to say that our knowledge of axioms is obtained by *intuition*, if the term is confined to 'those cases in which we necessarily apprehend the relations of things truly as soon as we conceive the objects distinctly'.[1]

To Mill, on the other hand, it was equally plain, while he was dealing with Whewell at any rate, that the first principles of mathematics are 'experimental truths' or 'generalizations from experience'. The proposition, for example, That two straight lines cannot enclose a space is 'an induction from the evidence of our senses'. In support of this contention he urges that whether or not axioms are self-evident, they are at any rate evident from experience. He then goes on to argue that having this evidence, it is unnecessary to suppose them to have any other; and in the course of his argument he is at particular pains to deny that any importance is to be attributed to the peculiar feeling of necessity that attaches to them.

'There is no more generally acknowledged fact in human nature', Mill holds, 'than the extreme difficulty at first felt in conceiving anything as possible which is in contradiction to long-established and familiar experience. And this difficulty is a necessary result of the fundamental laws of the human mind.' As then Whewell exhorts those who do not recognize the distinction between necessary and contingent propositions to study geometry, so Mill advises those who do to study the laws of association. He is convinced that nothing more than a moderate familiarity with these laws is required 'to dispel the illusion which ascribes a peculiar necessity to our earliest inductions from experience, and measures the possibility of things in themselves by the human capacity of conceiving them'. And it is along these lines that he meets Whewell's

[1] Whewell, *Mechanical Euclid*, pp. 181 ff.

argument that a belief in axioms cannot be derived from experience because we recognize their truth as soon as we distinctly conceive them. Mill admits the fact but denies the inference. The reason, he says, why axioms 'may be learnt from the idea only, without referring to the fact, is that in the process of acquiring the idea we have learnt the fact'. Thus (as Bain puts it) we cannot 'have the full meaning of straightness without going through a comparison of straight lines among themselves and with their opposites'; and one result of this comparison is that straightness in two lines is seen to be incompatible with enclosing a space.[1]

6. So far, then, as Mill was satisfied to assert an experiential theory of mathematics, it is easy enough to define his position in relation to Stewart and to Whewell, who were the authors of the principal alternative theories of the time. On the one hand, Mill was as convinced as Whewell that in some sense or other the first principles of mathematics, and more particularly of geometry, must be regarded as claiming truth; and he could not be any more sympathetic than Whewell to the hypothetical theory of Stewart. On the other hand he differs profoundly from Whewell regarding the way in which these first principles claim truth. For Whewell (as for Kant) mathematical propositions relate primarily to the forms of the mind and only secondarily to the objects of experience in so far as they have been impressed by the forms of mind. But for Mill, *in the second round of the debate at least*, mathematical propositions relate immediately and exclusively to the objects of experience.

We have now, however, to face the fact, which Mill himself never faced, that he was not entirely happy about the experiential theory. When Whewell had objected that experimental verification of the axioms of geometry is unattainable because we never have experience of the points and lines with which they are concerned, Mill had thought it

[1] *Logic*, ii. 5. 5 and 6.

sufficient to reply that we have, at any rate, experience of series of objects which approximate more and more closely to these points and lines.[1] But his position regarding definitions requires him to go further than this. Holding 'that what apparently follows from a definition follows in reality from an applied assumption that there exists a real thing conformable thereto', he now has to assert the actual existence of precisely these points and lines that Euclid speaks of; and this is more than he is prepared to do.

This assumption in the case of the definitions of geometry [he says] is not strictly true: there exist no real things exactly conformable to the definitions. There exist no points without magnitude; no lines without breadth, nor perfectly straight; no circles with all their radii exactly equal; nor squares with all their angles perfectly right. It will perhaps be said that the assumption does not extend to the actual, but only to the possible, existence of such things. I answer that, according to any test we have of possibility, they are not even possible. Their existence, so far as we can form any judgment, would seem to be inconsistent with the physical constitution of our planet, at least, if not of the universe.[2]

Hence in view of this difficulty Mill now turns away from the experiential theory and seeks refuge in the hypothetical theory of Dugald Stewart which he had previously rejected.

7. Stewart, he still thinks, was wrong in identifying the

---

[1] Though experience furnishes us with no lines so unimpeachably straight that two of them are incapable of enclosing the smallest space, nevertheless it does present us, Mill holds, 'with gradations of lines possessing less and less either of breadth or of flexure; of which series the straight line of the definitions is the ideal limit'. Observation, moreover, shows that 'just as much and as nearly, as the straight lines of experience approximate to having no breadth or flexure, so much and so nearly does the space-enclosing power of any two of them approach to zero'. Hence Mill concludes that we are justified in inferring from experience that if the lines had no breadth or flexure at all, as Euclid supposed, they would enclose no space. Ibid. ii. 5. 4, footnote.

[2] Ibid. ii. 5. 1. In the earlier editions Mill's statement was even stronger. He has 'false' instead of 'not strictly true' in the first sentence. This is the sort of change that Jevons complained about.

first principles of geometry with definitions. They are not definitions but postulates; but for all that they are still hypotheses; and, although in fact they are not, they might be, *arbitrary* hypotheses. Thus systems of propositions, as complicated as those of geometry, were deduced from false assumptions by Ptolemy and Descartes in their attempts to explain the solar system. Sometimes 'the same thing is knowingly done, as when the falsity of an assumption is demonstrated by a *reductio ad absurdum*'. Consequently Mill concludes that 'the opinion of Dugald Stewart regarding the foundations of geometry is substantially correct; that it is built on hypotheses: and that it owes to this alone, the peculiar certainty supposed to distinguish it'.[1]

But this position, again, is an impossible one for Mill. His fundamental conviction regarding mathematics is that, in view of its enormous utility in the development of science, it 'cannot be supposed to be conversant with non-entities'. But Stewart's theory of mathematics amounts to declaring that it is, or at least may be, so concerned. Hence although Mill allows that it might form 'a highly useful intellectual exercise' to trace the consequences of purely arbitrary hypotheses, he cannot bring himself to recognize that mathematics is actually of this nature. And his uncertainty over the whole matter is shown again by the fearful muddle he gets into regarding the term *hypothesis in the third round of the debate.*

For Stewart the first principles of geometry are hypotheses because they are *not asserted* to be true; and this is sometimes Mill's meaning. But he also says that they are hypotheses because they are not *in fact* true; and then he is led to identify *hypotheses* with *fictions*. 'The hypothetical element in the definitions of geometry', he says, 'is the assumption that what is very nearly true is exactly so. This unreal exactitude might be called a fiction as properly as an hypothesis.' It is with this

[1] *Logic*, ii. 6. 4; ii. 5. 1.

meaning of hypothesis in mind that Mill arrives at the conclusion that some at least of the principles of geometry are
not hypotheses because they are exactly true. The final
consequence of this confusion is the preposterous passage
which, read literally, asserts that the conclusions of geometry
are certain *because* the premisses are false. 'The conclusions',
says Mill, 'are only true on certain suppositions which are,
or ought to be approximations to the truth, but are seldom,
if ever, exactly true; and to *this* hypothetical character is to be
ascribed the peculiar certainty which is inherent in demonstration.'[1]

8. The trouble with Mill's treatment of mathematics in the
Logic is, then, that he could not make up his mind between
the experiential and the hypothetical theories. To begin
with he asserts the experiential theory; then he asserts the
hypothetical theory; then, again, he tries to have it both ways
by attributing a categorical character to the hypotheses of
Stewart with deplorable results. But it is equally evident that
this zigzag course is not pursued by Mill out of mere caprice.
He asserts the experiential theory because he is convinced
that mathematics cannot be supposed to be concerned with
nonentities. He asserts the hypothetical theory because he
has reluctantly to admit that many mathematical propositions
can only be regarded as false if they are predicated of the facts
which lie upon the surface of experience.

Thus what Mill really requires, it would seem, is a theory
which somehow combines the positive truth which he sees in
the experiential theory with the negative truth which he sees
in the hypothetical theory. It seems plain enough, moreover,
that the only theory capable of satisfying both these conditions
is the realist theory to which he subscribed in his later years
and which, although scarcely noticed in the *Logic*, is the only
theory consistent with his doctrine of induction. For seeing
that many of the propositions of mathematics are false when

---

[1] Ibid. ii. 5. 1, footnote; ii. 5. 3; ii. 6. 1.

they are predicated of the immediate object of sense experience; seeing also that Mill was determined to predicate them of something; the only course left to him was to predicate them of a set of entities which underlie, but do not themselves appear upon, the surface of experience.

Nor, when Mill has reached this point, is it necessary for him to postulate a special set of mathematical entities for this purpose. He has already recognized the existence of one such set of transcendent entities in the forces of physics. He has also recognized that in the work of Newton physics and mathematics are scarcely distinguishable. It is not surprising, therefore, that at the end—*in the fourth round of his debate about mathematics*—Mill should have endorsed in its regard a realist theory which is scarcely distinguishable from his realist theory of physics.

9. 'Nature as it falls within our ken', according to Mill, 'is composed of a multitude of forces of which the origin (at least the immediate origin) is different, and the effects of which on our senses are extremely different.' But all these forces, he argues, agree in producing motions in space and are therefore amenable to the laws of extension, while the laws of extension in their turn are reducible to the laws of number. Hence the reality underlying appearances, as Mill finally conceives it, becomes a sort of inverted hierarchy in four levels; and it is in terms of this thoroughly platonic conception that Mill proceeds to elucidate the functions of mathematics in modern science. At the base, supporting the rest of the laws of nature, are the laws of number; above them are the laws of extension; above them again are the laws of motion; finally, on top, immediately underlying the surface of experience, are the other laws of the universe.

It is because reality is so constituted, Mill tells us, that we are indebted to mathematics for all that we know of the great cosmic forces of gravitation and light, heat, and electricity. It is for the same reason that mathematics provides us with 'the one complete type and model of the investigation of nature by deductive reasoning', namely, Newton's discovery of the laws of the solar system. Consequently Mill argues, in opposition to Hamilton but in complete agreement with Plato, that nobody who is ignorant of mathematics can possibly have an adequate conception of human knowledge as 'an organic whole'.[1]

Pure mathematics [says this unexpected Mill] first gave us this conception: applied mathematics extends it to the realm of physical nature. Applied mathematics shows that not only the truths of abstract number and extension, but the external facts of the universe which we apprehend by our senses form, at least in a large part of all nature, a web similarly tied together. We are able by reasoning from a few fundamental truths to explain and predict the phenomena of material objects; and what is still more remarkable, the fundamental truths themselves were found out by reasoning; for they are not such as are obvious to the senses, but had to be inferred by a mathematical process from a mass of minute details which alone came within the direct reach of human observation.[2]

10. It would, perhaps, be going too far to say that these statements represent Mill's real convictions about mathematics. They are, after all, extracted from two quite short passages in the *Examination of Hamilton* and the *St. Andrews Address*; and anybody who chooses to maintain the orthodox view of Mill's teaching (which is also his own) can cite a far larger number and variety of statements from the *Logic*, the *Autobiography*, and the *Examination of Hamilton*.[3] Let us say then, in Mill's own language, not that he finally adheres, but

[1] *Examination of Hamilton*, pp. 619 ff.
[2] *St. Andrews Address*, p. 48.
[3] Including the famous footnote in which Mill maintained 'that the reverse of the most familiar principles of arithmetic and geometry might have been made conceivable, even to our present mental faculties if those faculties had co-existed with a totally different constitution of external nature'. *Examination of Hamilton*, pp. 89 ff.

that he has a tendency to adhere to a realist theory of mathematics. For we can then point not only to the evidence of these statements themselves but also to the peculiar incoherence of Mill's other statements about mathematics. We can also draw attention to the fact that a realist theory of mathematics is the only theory compatible with his realist account of the laws of causation. Finally we can quote a case precisely parallel to that of mathematics in which Mill's tendency to realism was actually consummated while he was writing the *Logic*.

It was Mill's contention, while he was dealing with induction, that the great majority of the ultimate laws of nature are causal laws, since it is only so far as they are causal laws that the canons of induction are applicable to them. He had no difficulty, moreover, in showing that a great many uniformities of co-existence, as well as of succession, are explicable as corollaries of causal laws. 'High water at any point on the earth's surface, and high water at the point diametrically opposite to it', for example, 'are effects uniformly simultaneous, resulting from the direction in which the combined attractions of the sun and moon act upon the waters of the ocean.' Nevertheless Mill does recognize that there are some uniformities of co-existence which cannot be accounted for in this way. Such are the first principles of mathematics. Such again are the ultimate laws of kinds by means of which we infer that certain properties will be found whenever other properties are found.

We perceive, for instance, water. We recognize it to be water by certain of its properties. Having recognized it, we are able to affirm of it innumerable other properties; which we could not do unless it were a general truth that the set of properties by which we identify the substance as water, always have [*sic*] those other properties conjoined with them.[1]

It appears, then, that by the time Mill had completed his *Logic* he had come to recognize that there is such a thing as

[1] *Logic*, iii. 22. 1 and 2.

natural classification as distinct from *artificial* classification. 'There are', he says, 'distinctions of kind; distinctions not consisting in a given number of definite properties, plus the effects which follow from those properties, but running through the whole nature of the things so distinguished.' He even goes so far as to speak of kinds as 'classes between which there is an impassable barrier'. But this had not always been Mill's view of classification and indeed he was only converted to it, as he tells us, while he was actually writing the *Logic*.

> In working out the logical theory of those laws of nature which are not laws of causation, nor corollaries of such laws, I was led [he says] to recognize kinds as realities in nature and not mere distinctions for convenience, a light which I had not obtained when the First Book was written, and which made it necessary to modify and change several chapters of that Book.[1]

Now the doctrine that kinds are 'mere distinctions for convenience' is, of course, the nominalist theory of classification and we know pretty well what Mill made of it because it is the theory expounded in his early review of Whately. But the doctrine that kinds are 'realities in nature' is the realist view. Thus Mill is saying here that while he was actually writing the *Logic* he deliberately switched from a nominalist to a realist theory of classification in order to square his teaching with his cosmology. What I am suggesting is that in regard to mathematics he needed not ten but forty years in order to do this.

11. But why then did he take so long? The answer to this question, as to many similar questions about Mill is, I believe, that he was led astray by controversial zeal. For the previous two centuries political reformers in Europe had been impressed, and indeed obsessed, by the extent to which a ruling class was able to pervert the minds of a people by slogans disseminated from the pulpit and echoed in the nursery. It

---

[1] Ibid. iv. 7. 4; *Autobiography*, p. 187.

appeared to them that the people must behave more reasonably (that is, more in accordance with their own interests)
if they were taught to see things as they really are, instead of
(in Locke's phrase) 'through other men's spectacles'. Thus
they were bound to view with suspicion any philosopher who
proposed to erect the principles he found in his own mind
into standards for the judgement of reality. This suspicion
was bound to be heightened if the philosopher was otherwise
of a conservative or reactionary turn of mind; and the radical
reformers of Mill's time were faced by an almost perfect example of this type of philosopher in Whewell.

Although Whewell is almost forgotten now he cut a very
considerable figure in the early Victorian period. When Mill
published his *Logic* he was Master of Trinity College and
Professor of Moral Philosophy at Cambridge. He was also
the leading authority on tidology in England and the arbiter
of her scientific terminology. (It was he, for instance, who
suggested the use of the terms *anode*, *cathode*, and *ions* to
Faraday.) The most eminent men paid tribute to his en-
cyclopaedic mind. In Herschel's opinion, 'a more wonderful
variety and amount of knowledge was perhaps never accumu-
lated by any man'. Macaulay credited him with even more
information than he himself possessed. According to a widely
circulated quip of Sydney Smith's—'Science was his *forte*,
omniscience his foible.' Such a man was bound to attract the
attention of a zealous young radical like John Mill. Outside
science, he was the champion of all the vested interests that
the utilitarians regarded as obstacles in the path of progress—
the established universities, the established church, and the
established constitution; and, in the opinion of the utilitarians
he constantly misused his immense scientific reputation to
protect them.

Moreover Mill had other reasons for being interested in
Whewell. He was indebted to Whewell's *History of the Inductive Sciences* for the comprehensive view of the physical

sciences which enabled him to write about induction; and he proposed to be indebted to him in another way in regard to another book. 'During the rewriting of the *Logic*', he says in the *Autobiography*, 'Dr. Whewell's *Philosophy of the Inductive Sciences* made its appearance; a circumstance fortunate for me, as it gave me a full treatment of the subject by an antagonist and enabled me to present my views with greater clearness and emphasis.' Mill was the more disposed to take advantage of this opportunity because he thought, from observation of Whewell's 'polemical propensities' in other cases, that he would probably do something to bring the *Logic* into notice by a prompt reply to this attack on his opinions.[1] This calculation, however, miscarried. Whewell had had his eye on young Mill for some time and he had no intention whatever of being used by him for publicity purposes. So although he read the book as soon as it appeared and privately praised it with faint damns, he made no public reply until seven years later, just in time for Mill to answer him in the third edition of the *Logic*. Nor is this the only way in which Mill's plans in regard to Whewell may be said to have miscarried; for in his anxiety to controvert Whewell on as many topics as possible, Mill was sometimes led to concentrate on peripheral elements in them to the detriment of central issues; and this I suggest is notably the case in regard to his theory of mathematics.

[1] *Autobiography*, pp. 188 f.

X

CONCLUSION

1. IT has often been noted as a peculiarity of modern philosophy that it subordinates all other problems to the problem of knowledge. Instead of inquiring directly into the nature of things, as the ancients were accustomed to do, the moderns begin (and frequently end) by seeking the appropriate method of inquiry in this sphere and that. The extent to which this approach to philosophy had become standardized in the nineteenth century is well exemplified in the commonly received doctrine of the two schools which is discussed in Chapter IV. It is by way of a legacy from this doctrine that we still tend to think of the distinction between empiricists and rationalists as the deepest that divides philosophers.

It has also been noted from time to time, however, that in approaching the problems of philosophy in this way, the moderns are in grave danger of arguing in a circle. On the one hand, they are bound to profess a good deal of ignorance regarding the objects under investigation; otherwise it would be pointless to bother about devising a method to investigate them. On the other hand, it is difficult to see how a method can be approved as appropriate to a class of objects except on the basis of some fairly large assumptions regarding them. The danger of circular argument here is greatly increased by the fact that modern philosophers have not usually found it easy to realize and state the precise nature and extent of the assumptions on which they have approved their methods. The case of Mill is particularly instructive in this respect in that he has managed to persuade several generations of philosophers to ignore the real foundations of some of his most important doctrines.

2. Mill always repudiated the notion that he was an empiricist, since that would imply, according to his understanding of the term, that he believed that knowledge must always be unsystematic and uncertain. But he always insisted at the same time that he was an adherent of the school of experience.

As to the fundamental difference of opinion respecting the sources of our knowledge [he says, for instance], we here content ourselves with a bare statement of our opinion. It is that the truth on this much debated question lies with the school of Locke and of Bentham. The nature and laws of things in themselves, or of the hidden causes of the phenomena which are the objects of experience appear to us radically inaccessible to the human faculties. We see no ground for believing that anything can be the object of our knowledge except our experience, and what can be inferred from our experience by the analogies of experience itself.[1]

But although such declarations as these have always seemed to Mill's commentators (as they did to Mill himself) to define the central features of his philosophical position, they are completely at odds with the assertions that he makes in his cosmology, where, indeed, he assumes a familiarity with the hidden causes of phenomena unrivalled by any rationalist. 'Nature', he says for example, 'means the sum of all phenomena, together with the causes which produced them; including not only all that happens but all that is capable of happening; *the unused capabilities of causes* being as much a part of the idea of Nature as those which take effect.'[2] Nor is it possible to regard these assertions as mere aberrations on Mill's part, without substantial effect on the body of his philosophy. On the contrary, Mill's whole conception of science, and consequently of induction, is based upon them. He always insisted that the phenomena which appear upon the surface of experience must be explained by referring them to their genesis in the underlying laws of nature. In order, therefore, to compare Mill's position here

[1] *Dissertations*, i. 409.   [2] *Three Essays on Religion*, p. 5.

with that of his contemporaries, it would seem necessary to compare his theory of explanation with theirs. It is also upon this basis, as I believe, that it is most instructive to compare Mill's position here with that which he takes up in other parts of his philosophy.

3. On the face of it a description answers the question, how? an explanation the question, why? Thus while Kepler, as it is frequently said, described *how* the planets move, it was left to Newton to explain *why* they move. But it is open to anybody to deny that there is a genuine distinction here; or again, if its genuineness is admitted, it may be interpreted in more than one way; and then it appears that there are three positions here which had powerful support in the early nineteenth century.

According to the *first* position, there is a genuine difference between description and explanation since the question, how? may be answered by the statement of uniformities among events, while the question, why? invites us to consider the causes of events. But the only intelligible cases of causation, it is argued, are to be found in instances of volition. In the last resort, therefore, a cause has to be defined (as Reid defined it) as 'a being that produces a change by the exercise of power'. Hence to explain a change it is necessary to make some reference to such a being. Where no such finite being is available, an infinite being must be postulated. Consequently it is held that while the question, how? calls for the statement of natural laws, the question, why? will inevitably lead us beyond the natural to the supernatural.

In England this was the view of most of the theologians of the time (Martineau is a good example), of some of the literary men (like Carlyle), and of a surprising number of scientists. Herschel provided an almost official statement of it in his presidential address to the British Association for the Advancement of Science in 1845. 'The Great First Agent', he declared, 'may lay down a rule of action for himself and that rule may become known to men by observation of its uniformity; but constituted as our minds are, and having that conscious knowledge of causation, which is forced upon us by the reality of the distinction between intending a thing and doing it, we can never substitute the Rule for the Act.'[1] Consequently Herschel, like Carlyle, regarded any scientist who attempts to go beyond description as usurping the functions of the theologian and building theories to dispense with God.

The *second* position is that of Mill for whom, as for Plato, the distinction between description and explanation is based on the distinction between a phenomenal world of ' actual results' and a real world of 'tendencies'. True statements about the former (like Kepler's laws of planetary motion) are called empirical laws, while true statements about the latter (like Newton's laws of motion) are laws of nature. But according to Mill there is an important difference between the kind of truth claimed by these statements which qualifies one of them to answer the question, how? and the other the question, why? Empirical laws only happen to be true because of the collocations of fact which obtain in this world while laws of nature, being independent of such collocations, will be true of all possible worlds (Chap. V).

In the *third* place it may be held that there is no difference between description and explanation except, perhaps, in degree of generality. The question, why? therefore will have no meaning distinct from the question, how? Consequently we can never have any rational grounds for believing in the existence of anything but natural laws and natural events. This is the position laid down for the positivists by Comte; and, like Mill, he illustrates his contention by reference to the doctrine of gravitation. Although we commonly say this doctrine *explains* the phenomena of the universe, all that it really does, according to Comte, is to *describe* them in terms of the constant tendency of atoms towards each other in

[1] Herschel, *Essays*, pp. 676 f.

direct proportion to their masses and in inverse proportion to the squares of their distances. Hence he maintains that we know, and can know, nothing of the force of gravity in itself. Theologians and metaphysicians, indeed, may imagine and refine about such questions but positive philosophers reject them.[1]

Thus Comte agrees with the volitionists in identifying the distinction between description and explanation with the distinction between science and theology. But he then goes on to identify it, further, with the distinction between the knowable and the unknowable. Consequently he considers the theory of Newton to be as descriptive as the laws of Kepler; and beyond the sort of thing they both say there is, he holds, nothing to be said.

4. The most explicit recognition of the importance of this threefold way of understanding the meaning of *explanation* is also to be found in a well-known doctrine of Comte's. According to Comte, it is a fundamental law of human intelligence that the leading conceptions of our knowledge, in all its branches, are destined to pass through three different stages. At the theological state, men suppose all events to be produced by the immediate action of supernatural beings; at the metaphysical stage, they refer them to abstract forms or forces; at the positive stage, they are content to discover their laws, that is, their invariable relations of succession and resemblance. Thus Comte holds that there are three and only three possible systems of philosophy, which he calls the theological or fictitious, the metaphysical or abstract, and the positive or scientific respectively. And these systems may be regarded as the correlatives of the current theories of explanation: the theological system is the correlative of the first theory, the metaphysical system of the second, the positive system of the third.

---

[1] Comte, *Positive Philosophy* (Bohn Edition, trans. Harriet Martineau), i. 5 f.

Comte cannot, however, be given much credit for the way he describes these systems. So far as the nineteenth century is concerned, there is no ground whatever for identifying the scientific with the positive way of looking at things. On the contrary, there is every ground for identifying it with the metaphysical. Thus, correcting Comte, we should speak, I suggest, of the metaphysical or abstract or scientific system as contrasted with the positive or experiential; or if more traditional language is preferred, we may equally well speak of the realist as contrasted with the nominalist system.

Then, again, Comte's description of the theological or fictitous mode of thought is altogether too tendentious. Fictitious, perhaps, it may be when it comes to referring all events to the actions of supernatural beings. But it is not so easy to regard as fictitious the belief, in which we are all apt to indulge, that human actions are to be ascribed to human beings. Yet the philosophers of this way of thinking were as much concerned to defend the latter way of speaking as the former. Their central contention, indeed, was that the latter way of speaking would finally be found to be indefensible unless the former was also indulged in. That is why the principal group of British philosophers who insisted on the validity of this sort of explanation—the Scottish school which was pioneered by Reid and headed in Mill's time by Hamilton—claimed to be the champions of common sense. While they were not, moreover, very successful in making out their case, they were certainly correct in holding that philosophy in their time was badly in need of an adequate defence of human agency. It still is.

Nor is Comte's bias apparent only in the names he gives to these three modes of thought. It is also apparent in his assertion that they follow each other in a regular order in time— the theological or volitional appearing first, the metaphysical or abstract next, and the positive or experiential last. There is little evidence of any such progression in the nineteenth century. While some men advanced from a volitional to a scientific and thence to a positive position, others felt themselves constrained to retreat in the opposite direction. But the most usual case was that of the men (like Mill) who attempted to combine a regular allegiance to the scientific theory of explanation with an occasional allegiance to the other two theories. Nor is it difficult to understand why this should be so; for the fact is that with all its magnificent achievements the metaphysical theory is thoroughly unstable in two directions. On the one hand, in regard to ethics and politics, it tends, by way of reaction, to provoke a return to the volitionist theory. On the other hand, in regard to theory of knowledge, it tends to fall of its own weight over into the positivist theory.

5. On the metaphysical system, as expounded by Mill, the nature of anything (like fire or water) is 'the aggregate of its powers or properties'. By the powers or properties of a thing he understands 'the modes in which it acts on other things and in which other things act upon it'; or, as he also says, 'its entire capacity of exhibiting phenomena'. Consequently he holds that Nature in the abstract is 'the aggregate of the powers and properties of all things . . . including not only all that happens but all that is capable of happening; the unused capabilities of causes being as much a part of the idea of Nature as those which take place'.

Nor does Mill think it necessary to modify this notion of Nature in any way in order to allow for the actions of human beings.

Art [he says] is as much Nature as anything else. . . . We move objects and by this simple change of place, natural forces previously dormant are called into action and produce the desired effect. Even the volition which designs, the intelligence which controls, and the muscular force which executes these movements are themselves powers of Nature. . . . All our actions are done through, and in obedience to, some one or many of Nature's physical or mental laws.[1]

[1] *Three Essays on Religion*, pp. 5 f., 64.

Thus Mill's metaphysical conception of Nature leads to a thoroughly naturalistic view of man; and to a large extent the problem of unravelling the tangled skein of Mill's philosophy is a question of tracing the consequences of this view. In the sphere of practice, it leads to the conclusion that in the last resort human beings, like physical things, must be regarded merely as areas within which laws of nature operate and interact; in the sphere of knowledge, it leads to the conclusion that we can never have any immediate knowledge of these laws but only of their effects upon us; and both these consequences are explicitly endorsed by Mill. The former is expounded in his doctrine of determinism or, as he prefers to say, of circumstances; the latter in his doctrine of the relativity of knowledge. Nevertheless Mill was unable to accept either of these doctrines in their entirety and his failure to do so is responsible for practically everything that is interesting and important in his philosophy.

6. It was in his early manhood—during the period that culminated in 'the dry heavy dejection of the melancholy winter 1826–27'—that the moral difficulty inherent in the naturalistic view of man was most acutely felt by Mill. He was then twenty years old and he had been working extremely hard all his life—first at being educated by his father and then at youthful propaganda and self-education. On top of that, he had already begun his successful career with the East India Company. There is no doubt that he had overworked. But it is equally plain that it was some hitch or impediment in the work, not its mere excess, that had caused his breakdown. He himself felt that the system of ideas in which he had been brought up did not satisfy all the needs of his nature; and at the centre of his discontent he was conscious of a deep dissatisfaction with the Benthamite dogma of determinism.

During the later returns of my dejection [he confesses in the *Autobiography*], the doctrine of what is called philosophical necessity weighed on my existence like an incubus. I felt as if I was scientifically proved to be the helpless slave of antecedent circumstances; as if my character and that of all others had been formed for us by agencies beyond our control, and was wholly out of our own power. I often said to myself, what a relief it would be if I could disbelieve the doctrine of the formation of character by circumstances; and remembering the wish of Fox respecting the doctrine of resistance to governments, that it might never be forgotten by kings nor remembered by subjects, I said, that it would be a blessing if the doctrine of necessity could be believed by all *quoad* the character of others, and disbelieved in regard to their own.[1]

Nor in spite of much painful pondering did Mill ever succeed in producing a satisfactory solution of the problem. On his premises, indeed, it is an insoluble problem. The doctrine of the formation of character by circumstances, as Mill understood it, is an inference from the universal Law of Causation. It amounts, therefore, to the assertion that human behaviour is determined by 'the causes called motives according to as strict laws as those which exist in the world of mere matter'.[2] Hence, on this view, the human being cannot be regarded as having any more individuality than the physical thing. He will be simply an area within which various laws of appetite resolve themselves according to a principle of the composition of motives strictly analogous to the principle of the composition of physical forces. Mill himself draws this conclusion quite explicitly when he is attempting to lay the foundations of a scientific sociology (Chap. V).

But Mill also wishes to hold that a man is not compelled, 'as by a magic spell', to obey any particular motive. He therefore suggests that every man has 'to a certain extent' a power of altering his own character, that is, the congeries of appetites which renders him susceptible to the influence of certain causes or motives; and in making this suggestion it is evident that Mill regards the human being as something quite differ-

---

[1] *Autobiography*, p. 143.   [2] *Logic*, ii. 5. 8 footnote.

ent from an area upon which various lines of force converge. Mill has now, in fact, completely reversed the relation between the man and his motives. According to the doctrine of circumstances it is the motives which make the man; according to the doctrine of self-formation it is the man who makes the motives. He is now a person 'who feels that his habits or his temptations are not his master but he theirs; who even in yielding to them knows that he could resist'; and the plain fact of the matter is that the view of the universe which Mill inherited from Bentham and his father did not permit him to recognize the existence of such a person.[1]

In the upshot Mill contrives to retain both these views of human nature by expounding them in different parts of his philosophy. The exposition of the naturalistic or scientific view is largely confined to the heavier treatises on scientific method like the *Logic*; that of the romantic or self-formative view to the more popular essays on ethics like the essay on *Liberty* (Chap. II). Nevertheless, Mill's writings are spotted with reminders of the inconsistency between these two views of man; and this is nowhere more apparent than in his treatment of politics where he could never make up his mind whether his final allegiance was to the principle of utility which is derived from the naturalistic view or to the principle of individuality which is derived from the volitionist view (Chap. III).

7. The difficulties inherent in a naturalistic view of man appear in a rather different light when we turn from Mill's ethics and politics to his epistemology and logic. In the former we are concerned with his blind romantic revolt against determinism because of his inability to square its implications with the demands of morality. In the latter it is a question of tracing the consequences for knowledge of the fundamental dualism of his conception of Nature.

In accordance with Mill's general notion of Nature the

---

[1] Ibid. vi. 2. 2 and 3.

occurrence of knowledge, like any other occurrence, has to be explained by reference to the ways in which things act and react upon each other in accordance with the laws of their nature. It follows that we can never have any immediate knowledge of these things or their laws but only of their effects upon us. It also follows that these effects will be very different from their causes; for the causes are material forces, like the force of gravity, while their results, as known to us, being their effects on our minds, will be our states of consciousness. Thus, according to Mill, the only objects of which we have, or can have, immediate knowledge are our own ideas; and he is never tired consequently of proclaiming himself a subjective idealist of the school of Berkeley. But like the other exponents of the way of ideas (with the possible exception of Berkeley) he only arrives at this conclusion on the basis of his Newtonian cosmology (Chap. VII). Nor indeed is there anything noteworthy about Mill's version of the theory of ideas apart from the extraordinary obstinacy with which he refused to profit from the experience of his predecessors.

The new way of ideas initiated by Locke in the Royal Society atmosphere of the late seventeenth century had been succeeded in the eighteenth century by the philosophies of Hume, of Reid and the Scottish School, and of Hartley and Priestley. Hume traced and enjoyed the sceptical implications of Locke's principles. Reid found that he could neither accept Hume's conclusions nor deny that they followed from Locke's premisses; consequently he attempted to formulate a new position, leaning heavily upon the dictates of common sense, which was to make a particular appeal to Hamilton. Hartley and Priestley, however, continued to stand by Locke; they either ignored the difficulties raised by Hume or they assumed, without going into the matter very deeply, that these difficulties could be met without any radical revision of Locke's premisses; and it was from Hartley and Priestley, as he frequently acknowledges, that Mill derived the leading principles of his epistemology. The lengths to which he was prepared to go in following them are only too plainly apparent in his controversy with Hamilton who was his chosen antagonist on this subject.

8. When I concentrate my attention on the simplest act of perception [says Hamilton], I return from my observation with the most irresistible conviction of two facts, or rather two branches of the same fact—that I am—and that something different from me exists. In this act I am conscious of myself as the perceiving subject—and of an external reality as the object perceived; and I am conscious of both existences in the same indivisible moment of intuition.[1]

According to Mill, on the other hand, this duality of consciousness, although a fact of my experience now, cannot possibly be regarded as an ultimate fact. The only ultimate facts of the case, he holds, are the occurrence of sensations and their recurrence in groups in such a way that when one occurs it will tend, according to the laws of association, to reinstate the ideas of the other. Setting out from these premises he accordingly undertakes to show 'that there are associations naturally and even necessarily generated by the order of our sensations and of our reminiscence of sensations which, supposing no intuition of an external world to have existed in consciousness, would inevitably generate the belief and would cause it to be regarded as an intuition'. He also undertakes to show, although not quite so confidently, that a similar explanation may be given of our alleged intuition of ourselves.[2]

Thus, here again, in Mill's theory of perception we encounter the same mistrust of what is revealed upon the surface of experience that is such a prominent feature of his general theory of science. Here again there is the same appeal to ultimate facts, in the shape of sensations, and to underlying tendencies, in the shape of laws of association. Here again,

---

[1] Hamilton, *Discussions*, pp. 54 f.
[2] *Examination of Hamilton*, pp. 227, 265.

moreover, we find Mill attributing the same kind of horrid consequences to the theory of his opponent. Here again, to complete the similarity, it is necessary to protest against the tendentious account which he gives of his own theory.

The difference between his philosophy and Hamilton's, according to Mill, is not a mere matter of abstract speculation. 'It is full of practical consequences and lies at the foundation of all the greatest differences of opinion in an age of progress.' The practical reformer has continually to demand that changes be made in institutions which are supported by powerful and widely spread feelings. It is often an indispensable part of his argument to show that these feelings had their origins in circumstances and associations. There is, therefore, a natural hostility between him and a philosophy which deems intuition to be the voice of God—speaking with an authority higher than that of reason. Consequently, regarding the fame of Sir William Hamilton as 'the great fortress' of the intuitionist philosophy in Britain at this time, Mill considered it to be his duty, as a practical reformer, to undertake a critical examination of Hamilton's teaching. He always, moreover, regarded Hamilton's theory of perception as the core of that teaching.[1]

In fact, however, this statement of the case gives a completely misleading impression of the question at issue between Hamilton and Mill regarding perception. Both philosophers are engaged in an attempt to analyse experience. Both, again, assume that in such an analysis it is necessary to distinguish between the original and the acquired elements of experience. So far, then, as they both regard *intuition* as synonymous with *original experience*, they agree that there is such a thing as intuition. Thus the question at issue does not require us, as Mill suggests, to balance the claims of experience against those of intuition; it requires us rather to balance the claims of two different analyses of experience or, what amounts to

[1] *Autobiography,* pp. 232 f.

the same thing, two different interpretations of intuition. And the melancholy fact is that Hume had conclusively demonstrated the complete unacceptibility of Mill's analysis long before Mill made it.

9. So far as our belief in an external world is concerned, the great difficulty on Mill's principles is, as Hume pointed out, that 'mind has never anything present to it but the perceptions and cannot reach any experience of this connexion with objects'. Mill was well aware of this difficulty and was, in fact, fully prepared to admit that he could not prove the 'real externality' of anything beyond his own mind except, perhaps, other minds. Nevertheless he held that he could account for the whole of our actual notion of the external world by defining it as a 'Permanent Possibility of Sensation', since it was his opinion that we do not really believe in the existence of anything beyond mind although we think we do. 'If I am asked', he says, 'whether I believe in matter I ask whether the questioner accepts this definition of it. If he does, I believe in matter; and so do all Berkeleians. In any other sense than this, I do not. But I affirm with confidence that this conception of Matter includes the whole meaning attached to it by the common world, apart from philosophical, and sometimes from theological theories. The reliance of mankind on the real existence of visible and tangible objects, means reliance on the reality and permanence of Possibilities of visual and tactual sensations, when no such sensations are actually experienced.'[1]

But this doctrine, as has frequently been pointed out, is capable of two quite different interpretations. It may mean that there are permanent conditions outside the mind which are capable of causing sensations within it. Or it may mean that it is permanently possible for mind to feel certain sensations when certain purely mental conditions are satisfied. 'It

[1] Hume, *Enquiry concerning Human Understanding*, sect. xii, part i; Mill, *Examination of Hamilton*, p. 233.

may, in short, mean either a Permanent Possibility of *producing* the sensations, or a Permanent Possibility of *feeling* them.'[1] Moreover it owes its plausibility entirely to this ambiguity. Do you retain a disposition to believe in the existence of Matter independent of Mind, then Mill offers you Permanent Possibilities of Sensation which he afterwards identifies with Laws of Nature and endows with a reality far transcending that of mere sensation. Do you, as a strict Berkeleian, believe in the existence of nothing but Minds and States of Mind, then he is your man again, for apart from Mind he asserts only the possibilities of sensation, that is, of States of Mind. All that you need to satisfy the requirements of nearly everybody on this theory (except perhaps the Common Man who *will* continue to believe in tables and chairs) is a nice discrimination in the use of capital letters.

The snag is, of course, that in pretending to be all things to all men you are very liable to become something of a split personality yourself; and this, as Martineau has forcibly pointed out, is precisely what happened to Mill here.

On the one hand [Martineau says of Mill], we have found him resolving all our knowledge into self-knowledge; denying any cognitive access to either qualities or bodies external to us; and shutting us up with our own sensations, ideas and emotions. But, on the other hand, though we *know* nothing but the phenomena of ourselves we *are* nothing but phenomena of the world: the boast is vain of anything original in the mind: the sensations from which all within us begins are the results of *outward experience*. And thus we are landed in this singular result: our only sphere of cognizable reality is subjective: and *that* is generated from an objective world which we have no reason to believe exists. In our author's theory of *cognition*, the non-ego disappears in the ego; in his theory of *being*, the ego lapses into the non-ego. Idealist in the former, he is materialist in the latter.[2]

[1] W. H. S. Monck, *Sir William Hamilton*, p. 17.
[2] Martineau, *Essays*, iii. 520.

10. Nor is Mill any more succesful in providing an account of the knowing subject than of the objective world. There is no doubt about the sort of theory which should be given of mind on his principles. 'The true idea of the human mind', Hume puts it, 'is to consider it as a system of different perceptions or different existences which are linked together by the relation of cause and effect and mutually produce, destroy, influence and modify each other.' Up to a point, moreover, Mill appears happy enough about this theory of mind, particularly as he is able to formulate it in terms which run parallel to his theory of matter. 'The belief I entertain that my mind exists when it is not feeling, nor thinking, nor conscious of its own existence resolves itself', he says, 'into the belief of a Permanent Possibility of these states.' Hence he concludes that we may regard mind 'as nothing but a series of our sensations (to which must now be added our internal feelings) as they actually occur, with the addition of infinite possibilities of feeling requiring for their actual realization conditions which may or may not take place'.[1]

The difficulty is, however, that we are not only such a series of actual and possible states of mind. We are also aware of ourselves as being such a series. Thus, as Mill admits, 'we are reduced to the alternative of believing that the Mind, or Ego is something different from any series of feelings, or possibilities of them, or of accepting the paradox that something which *ex hypothesi* is but a series of feelings, can be aware of itself as a series'. And in the presence of these alternatives Mill frankly confesses that he is unable to come to any decision. 'I think', he says, 'by far the wisest thing we can do is to accept the inexplicable fact, without any theory as to how it takes place; and when we are obliged to speak of it in terms which assume a theory, to use them with a reservation as to their meaning.' In other words, Mill is unable to make anything of the notion of a knowing subject in associationist

[1] Hume, *Treatise*, i. 4. 6; Mill, *Examination of Hamilton*, p. 241.

terms and he is unwilling to try and make anything of it in any other terms. It is hard to imagine a more candid confession of intellectual bankruptcy; and the consequences of Mill's failure in this case are fully as serious as they were in the previous case. For when we turn from speculation to practice, the problem of reconciling flux and permanence in the knowing subject re-emerges as the problem of reconciling determinism and free will in the moral agent; and this is a problem, as Mill had already discovered, which is capable of preying on the mind.[1]

11. In one way Mill's logic is completely different from his epistemology since there is a novelty and freshness about the former which is completely lacking in the latter. In another way, however, Mill's treatment of the two subjects is astonishingly similar; for as in epistemology he was torn between the claims of materialism and of idealism, so in logic he sometimes endorses a realist and sometimes a nominalist theory of universals. In regard to induction he assumes that all particulars are expressions of underlying universals (Chap. V), and so he arrives at the conclusion that certainty is attainable by way of scientific experiment (Chap. VI). In regard to the syllogism, on the contrary, he maintains that universals are merely collections of particulars and he allows us to conclude, therefore, that all inference is uncertain (Chap. VIII).

Thus it is quite impossible in my opinion to defend the consistency of Mill's theories of induction and of the syllogism. Nevertheless it is not difficult, I believe, to understand how he came to make the transition from the one theory to the other. The universal laws of nature postulated in his theory of induction are lifted directly from his cosmology while the particulars postulated in his theory of the syllogism are the states of consciousness produced in us by these laws on this occasion and that. In the one case, Mill presents us with a

---

[1] *Examination of Hamilton,* pp. 247 f.

bird's-eye view of Nature appropriate to the scientist who has taken all knowledge for his domain. In the other case, he has taken account of the fact that from the bird's point of view we are merely creatures of Nature who can only be credited with a worm's-eye view of it (Chap. VII).

Nor are Mill's oscillations between these points of view apparent only in the way that he moves from his theory of induction to his theory of the syllogism. They are also apparent within his treatment of each of these topics. Although his theory of induction is predominantly realist, he sometimes lapses into a nominalist position there, as in some of his statements about causation. On the other hand, the nominalist theory of the syllogism usually associated with his name is balanced by an almost equally well-developed realist theory. Moreover, Mill's uncertainty about the ultimate premises of human knowledge becomes painfully apparent again when we attempt to disentangle the astonishing variety of statements that he makes about mathematics, which is a sort of buffer topic intermediate between induction and the syllogism. Although he always proclaims himself an experientialist in regard to mathematics he ends by endorsing a realist theory of the subject which is practically indistinguishable from his realist theory of physics (Chap. IX).

12. I submit, then, that we can discover a certain pattern in Mill's philosophy, provided we are prepared to discount many of the catchwords current about it. His more important philosophical writings divide into two groups—one relating to ethics and politics, the other to logic and scientific method—and in either case he was torn between two incompatible ways of treating his subject. In ethics he could not make up his mind whether his final allegiance was to the principle of utility or to the principle of individuality; in logic he sometimes endorses a realist and sometimes a nominalist theory of universals. But all the same it would be a mistake to regard all these tendencies as being equally influential in Mill's thought.

He was always a realist while he was in earnest about science; so far as he was intent, like Bentham, upon making something scientific out of politics, he was also a utilitarian; and there are few philosophers who have been more thoroughly in earnest about science than Mill. Hence in my opinion his scientific or metaphysical or realist theory of explanation should be regarded as the central conception of his philosophy.

Now if this is a correct estimate of Mill's position it does not seem difficult to understand the genesis of his inconsistencies. The unresolved conflict between the principles of utility and of individuality may be expected to issue in one set of inconsistencies; the conflict between his realist and his nominalist theory of universals in another. But at bottom it is always a question with Mill of reconciling a naturalistic view of man with the assumptions that we habitually make about ourselves and about other men when we are not investigating them scientifically. I mean the assumption, for instance, that human actions may be characterized as right or wrong and humans opinion as true or false; or the assumption, again, that in some sense or other human actions and human opinions are to be credited (or debited) to human beings.

Nor should we forget, as we smile at the inconsistencies into which Mill fell as he struggled with this question, that it is still an open question. The scientist with his bias towards a realist theory of universals is still unable to accept our claims to knowledge and to morality at their face value. So far as he continues to think scientifically he is still bound to regard them as mere appearances explicable in terms of an underlying reality of causal laws. Nobody has yet been able to show that if they are so explicable our claims to knowledge and morality may be regarded as having any validity. Yet how many men nowadays are prepared to assert that they are *not* so explicable?

INDEX

PRINTED IN GREAT BRITAIN
AT THE UNIVERSITY PRESS, OXFORD
BY CHARLES BATEY, PRINTER TO THE UNIVERSITY